"Bob Hostetler only gets better with every book. In *Life Stinks*, he shows how the world's reeking unfairness and brimstone breaths can be confronted by a holy halitosis, and the stenches of a daily grind sanctified into the very eau de Jesus."

> —**Leonard Sweet**, author of *Jesus: A Theography* and the E. Stanley Jones Professor of Evangelism at Drew Theological School at Drew University

"Bob Hostetler's work, like the book itself, is engaging and entertaining, lively and potent, evinces lots of reading, reflection, and a lovely wit. Hostetler's pointed applications will sometimes evoke an 'Amen,' and at other times a 'Yelp!' His illustrations meander through foibles and annoyances to issues of real personal pain—and all the while his pastoral experience is evident. 'Life Stinks'—but this book may help with the pain."

> —**Dr. Ronald B. Allen**, Senior Professor of Bible Exposition, Dallas Theological Seminary

"Strangely, Ecclesiastes is one of my favorite books of the Bible. It is honest. True to life. So down-to-earth, you feel the mud on your shoes as you walk through its pages. At times it sounds downright cynical. But while bluntly unmasking the futility of life, it also points to the source of hope. With customary insight and wit, Bob Hostetler helps us delve into the strange but wonderful wisdom of Ecclesiastes as it asks the questions the rest of the Bible was written to answer."

> —**Dr. David Faust**, president of Cincinnati Christian University

"It takes a big-hearted guy like Hostetler to show how the book of Ecclesiastes isn't cynical or world-weary at all but, well, as big-hearted and inspiring as Bob Hostetler. Not only do you get to know the author of some timeless biblical wisdom but you get to know a man who has lived his faith wisely and well."

> —**Rick Hamlin**, executive editor of Guideposts

"This is the most encouraging, interesting and applicable book on Ecclesiastes that I have ever read. I've always been impressed with Bob's ability to entertain while teaching, but I stand amazed at how he manages to deliver new insights into an ancient book that are fresh, relevant, and dare I say it, exciting! Prepare yourself for a humor-heavy, truth-filled, God-packed read that, if carefully applied, will lead to a life-changing experience that is both real and lasting."

—**Torry Martin**, actor, screenwriter, and creator of Wooten Bassett for "Adventures in Odyssey"

"Bob Hostetler has a knack for presenting life-changing truth in an entertaining and compelling way. He does it again with this book"

—**Mike Erre,** senior pastor of the First Evangelical Free Church of Fullerton, CA, and author of *Why the Bible Matters*

LIFE
STINKS

LIFE
STINKS
...AND THEN YOU DIE

LIVING
WELL
IN A SICK
WORLD

Bob Hostetler

LEAFWOOD
PUBLISHERS

LIFE STINKS . . . AND THEN YOU DIE

Living Well in a Sick World

LEAFWOOD
P U B L I S H E R S

Copyright © 2013 by Bob Hostetler

ISBN 978-0-89112-377-4
LCCN 2013024981

Printed in the United States of America

LIBRARY OF CONGRESS CATALOGING-IN-PUBLICATION DATA
Hostetler, Bob, 1958-
  Life stinks...and then you die : living well in a sick world / by Bob Hostetler.
    pages cm
  ISBN 978-0-89112-377-4
  1. Bible. Ecclesiastes--Criticism, interpretation, etc. 2. Life--Religious aspects--Christianity. I. Title.
  BS1475.52.H67 2013
  223'.806--dc23

                                                                                    2013024981

Cover design by Marc Whitaker   Interior text design by Sandy Armstrong, Strong Design

Leafwood Publishers is an imprint of Abilene Christian University Press
1626 Campus Court, Abilene, Texas 79601
1-877-816-4455   www.leafwoodpublishers.com

13 14 15 16 17 18 / 7 6 5 4 3 2 1

To my parents,

Vernon and Millie Hostetler

Contents

Acknowledgments

Thank you to my agent and friend, Steve Laube of the Steve Laube Agency, for representing me on this project.

Thank you to Dr. Leonard Allen, Gary Myers, Mary Hardegree, Robyn Burwell, and all the folks at Leafwood Publishers for seeing the value in this book and its message, and for the inestimable expertise that made it better at every point in the process.

Thank you to the prayer team whose faithful prayer support for me and for this project was felt throughout the process, and particularly at crucial points: Suzan Hughes, Dewey Hughes, Cheryl Johnson, Millie Merkel, Dave Merkel, Brad Newcomer, and Debbie Stacy. Your ministry to me and to the readers of this book is deeply appreciated.

Thank you also—as always—to the lovely Robin, my wife, my best friend, boon companion, confidante, lover, teacher, conscience, supporter, encourager, and muse.

LIFE'S JUST A BOWL OF CHERRIES. ROTTEN CHERRIES.

It begins with a single, beautiful butterfly. A monarch butterfly, or perhaps its look-alike, a viceroy.

The butterfly lands on the side mirror of a large SUV, setting off the car's anti-theft alarm. The noise startles a squirrel, which loses its perch on a branch and drops into a bowl of nuts or grapes next to a sunbathing woman. Frightened, she leaps up and screams, distracting the man across the street, who is washing his car. He inadvertently sprays the operator of a front loader, who loses control of his machine and launches a large rock into the air. The rock flies over a building and lands on the tongue of a boat trailer. The boat on the trailer flips into the air like a missile and crashes through the roof of a house as the home's resident stands at the curb fixing his mailbox. Hearing the clatter behind him, the man slowly turns around to see a gaping boat-shaped hole in the roof of his house. The television commercial ends with an announcer's voice: "Life comes at you fast. Nationwide. Investments. Retirement. Insurance."

That effective advertisement was one in a series of Nationwide Insurance commercials that ran for five years, each bearing the tag line, "Life comes at you fast." Some of the commercials featured celebrities such as MC Hammer, Fabio, and Kevin Federline. Many became big hits, and the series spawned numerous parodies on YouTube. By any measurement, the commercials were a success.

The ad campaign worked, of course, because the commercials were funny. But they also tapped into a nearly universally recognized truth: life does come at you fast. Sometimes blindingly fast. And it often leaves gaping holes and burning embers in its wake.

When Life Goes South

No one who has lived very long can deny that life is not all fun and games. It comes at you fast and often leaves a mark. That is the reason for the title of this book: *Life Stinks . . . and Then You Die*. But that's not to suggest that life lacks all pleasure. Not at all. There is much in life that is beautiful and wonderful—a baby's laugh, a friend's hug, a mountain lake, a pie pulled fresh from the oven. As songwriters Bob Thiele and George David Weiss wrote (and Louis Armstrong famously sang), many lovely features of this world—trees of green, red roses, "the bright blessed day," and "dark sacred night"—can prompt a person to think, "What a wonderful world."[1]

And, truth be told, many people do seem to skip blithely through the meadows of this world with nary a wound or scar. Day after day seems to shine on them. They wake up each morning with a smile on their faces. They meet and marry the person of their dreams. Their children are always clean and obedient. Their cars never break down, their friends never betray them, and their jobs never get "outsourced" or "downsized."

But it seems to me that most of those people are still quite young. The longer a person lives, the more pain he or she experiences. The older a person gets, the more tempting it is to become cynical. Jaded. Or, as some might put it, simply realistic.

Though I write full time these days, I have in my short lifetime been the pastor of four churches—one in southeast Ohio, one in northeast Ohio, and two in southwest Ohio. Being a pastor is, in some ways, like having a front row seat to life's highest highs and lowest lows. Pastors are present not only at jubilant events like baptisms and weddings, but also at less-happy moments in hospitals, nursing homes, and funeral homes.

I suppose I'll always remember July 4, 1985, when my wife and I were called to the hospital room of two dear friends. We expected to hear the news that Bud and Becky had welcomed their first child into the world. But we learned instead that their baby boy, whom they had named Jonathan, was stillborn. We cried together, cradled that tiny lifeless form in our arms, and held a bedside memorial service for that precious child—and for his parents' countless hopes and plans for him.

Another entry in my pastoral records is for a young man named Jason. Just weeks into his senior year of high school, eighteen-year-old Jason was killed in an automobile accident on his way to school. The honor student had planned to take his girlfriend to their senior homecoming celebration, which was to take place the next weekend.

Bill was a man in the church my wife and I had helped to start in Oxford, Ohio. He had recently moved to the area in secret, having escaped his former high position in a satanic coven in Pennsylvania. He found our church, became a follower of Jesus, and made many new friends. He was baptized on the Sunday before Christmas 2002. Just two months later, however, one of his new friends went to call on him at his apartment. Bill didn't answer. He had died of a massive heart attack in the middle of the night.

Those are just three examples of people with whom I have hurt and cried over the years. The worst of it is, their experiences are not unique. Many others could share tales of one heartbreak after another, stories of disease, divorce, depression, abuse, addiction, poverty, and pain. Even if your life has been largely pleasant and generally positive to date, you have certainly endured some painful experiences—if you are old enough to read this book, that is. And while those experiences may not yet have pierced your optimism and sunny disposition, you may someday wonder (as many others do) if it is possible to live well when life seems to curdle and sour. You may hunger for hope. For answers. For something more real and lasting than well-meaning platitudes.

That is what I hope to supply in the coming pages of this book. However, I won't be alone in that endeavor. I will rely on another guide, someone who experienced more life, wealth, and wisdom than I could ever claim.

Wiser Than Anyone

He lived roughly one thousand years before the birth of Jesus Christ. His father was king. And not just any king, but a man who molded a kingdom out of a bunch of fractious tribes and warring factions. The father's name was David; the son was given the name Solomon. The father was a shepherd, a poet, and a warrior; the son's very name was "peace," a form of the word *shalom*.

Upon the death of King David, Solomon became the king in Jerusalem, sometime around 970 BC. He reigned for forty years, presiding over a period in Israel's history that is routinely called the "Golden Age." His kingdom extended from the Euphrates River in present-day Syria to the Arabian Desert and the Gulf of Aqaba in the south. His crowning achievement was the construction of the Temple in Jerusalem. He was renowned for his wisdom, wealth, and accomplishment, some of which is described in 1 Kings 4:25–34:

> During the lifetime of Solomon, all of Judah and Israel lived in peace and safety. And from Dan in the north to Beersheba in the south, each family had its own home and garden.
>
> Solomon had 4,000 stalls for his chariot horses, and he had 12,000 horses.
>
> The district governors faithfully provided food for King Solomon and his court; each made sure nothing was lacking during the month assigned to him. They also brought the necessary barley and straw for the royal horses in the stables.
>
> God gave Solomon very great wisdom and understanding, and knowledge as vast as the sands of the seashore. In fact, his wisdom exceeded that of all the wise men of the East and the wise men of Egypt. He was wiser than anyone else, including Ethan the Ezrahite and the sons of Mahol—Heman, Calcol, and Darda. His fame spread throughout all the surrounding nations. He composed some 3,000 proverbs and wrote 1,005 songs. He could speak with authority about all kinds of plants, from the great cedar of Lebanon to the tiny hyssop that grows from cracks in a wall. He could also speak about animals, birds, small creatures, and fish. And kings from every nation sent their ambassadors to listen to the wisdom of Solomon.[2]

Some of King Solomon's proverbs are preserved in the book of Proverbs, in our Bible. At least one of his songs—the Song of Songs, or Song of Solomon—is also a part of our Bible. The ancient rabbis, as well as many more recent authorities, suggested that Song of Songs was written when Solomon was a young man, and Proverbs was written (and perhaps compiled) in the middle years of his life. But a third book is often considered to have been the product of Solomon's mind in his latter years, when he had seen it all, done it all, and bought the T-shirt, so to speak.

A Fine-Hammered Steel of Woe

The book of Ecclesiastes is often described as the strangest book of the Bible. George S. Hendry called it "disjointed in construction, obscure in vocabulary, and often cryptic in style."[3] F. C. Jennings referred to it as "an enigma" and an "arsenal" for attacks against the Bible as God's Word.[4] On the other hand, Herman Melville, in *Moby Dick*, praised it as "the truest of all books . . . the fine-hammered steel of woe."[5] And novelist Thomas Wolfe said, "Ecclesiastes is the greatest single piece of writing I have ever known."[6]

Dr. A. F. Harper says that "Ecclesiastes is . . . like a diary in which a man has recorded his impressions from time to time,"[7] and Dr. Charles Swindoll describes it as the journal of Solomon's "mid-life crisis."[8]

However, it is not universally agreed that Solomon wrote it. He is never identified by name in the book. Instead, the first verse ascribes the book to "the Teacher, son of David, king in Jerusalem."[9] It is a clear reference to Solomon, though some scholars say he couldn't have written the book, because of some of the words and phrasing it uses. In any case, there is no doubt that not only the first verse but the entire book refers to and relies on the life, wisdom, and experience of King Solomon.

The author is identified by a Hebrew word, *Qoheleth* (or Koheleth), which, when it was translated into Greek, became "Ecclesiastes," and in English is rendered "Teacher." Hendry explains:

> The word is connected with *qahal*, the public assem-
> bly, and it suggests the kind of wisdom delivered by the
> speaker to those in the outer court, as distinguished from
> the "hidden wisdom" which is known only to those who
> have been admitted to the mystery of God. (1 Cor. 2:7)[10]

It combines connotations of "prophet," "priest," and "king." But there
may also be a broader intention in the use of that word—and in the
way the entire book is presented, according to Ronald B. Allen,
senior professor of Bible exposition at Dallas Theological Seminary:

> Solomon might have written this wisdom book as a tract
> for other nations. . . . Solomon had entertained many dig-
> nitaries from other nations, including the queen of Sheba.
> The queen's questions concerning the basic meaning of
> life might have prompted him to write Ecclesiastes to
> teach the Gentiles about the living God.[11]

For all these reasons, I will most often refer to the author as *Qoheleth*
in these pages. In doing so, I hope to preserve the author's apparent
intention to evoke the king's wisdom and authority while simultaneously assuming an added aura of mystery and universality. I will
also conclude each of the chapters in this book with a prayer, to help
you apply and internalize the content of the preceding chapter at a
deeper level. I truly believe the inspired words of Ecclesiastes can
change your life, and those prayers are key to that process. I hope
you won't skip them. In fact, I hope you will do more than simply
read them. I invite you to take the time and thought to pray each
one, even aloud, because I believe that sincerely praying those words
(and, ideally, even adding to them, according to how the Holy Spirit
of God is moving you at that moment) will make you a partner with
God in applying his Word to your life and bringing about real and
lasting change, which is the purpose for which I write.

In any case, Ecclesiastes is of great value, and perhaps never more so than in this day and age, for people like you and me. Dr. John Paterson writes,

> It would have been a great pity and a serious loss if a book that is meant to be the Bible of all men made no reference or failed to deal with the mood of scepticism which is common to all men.[12]

Swindoll adds,

> I am pleased that we have this ancient book available today to set the record straight. All around us are people who are buying into [an] empty, horizontal, who-needs-God perspective. Their . . . whole frame of reference is humanistic. We see it lived out in soap operas every afternoon and on prime time every night. We hear it in political speeches. We learn it in the halls of academia, on the streets of any city.[13]

Is this life all there is? Is it best summed up as, "Life stinks . . . and then you die"? Is it inevitable for the potential and optimism of youth to falter and fade in the harsh light of disease, divorce, depression, abuse, addiction, poverty, and pain? Or is it possible to live well in spite of such dangers and disasters? Does the wisest man who ever lived have any wisdom to impart to us, thirty centuries later?

I think so. And I can't wait to show you why.

———— ～ ————

Lord God, I am ready. I am open. I am willing and waiting to hear your voice speaking to me through the words of Qoheleth. Please use this "fine-hammered steel of woe"—this book of Ecclesiastes—as well as the pages of this book that follow and the time and attention I invest in them to shine a light on my experiences, struggles, disappointments, defeats—and victories. Use this book to teach me how to live well when life seems to curdle and sour. Use these pages to speak far more than well-meaning platitudes— speak your truth and your will to my listening ears and waiting heart. Impart hope. Give insight. Meet needs—not only my needs in this moment, but those that you know will arise in the days and weeks and months ahead. Guide me through this book so that when I have finished reading it, it will have been far, far more than an interesting intellectual exercise. Please make it a life-changing experience. In Jesus' name, amen.

WHAT GOES AROUND,
GOES AROUND

Some people are always happy, always positive, always seeing a silver lining in every cloud.

Those people make me sick.

Don't get me wrong (though I know it's hard not to after a comment like that). I like to think I'm a positive person. I'm a glass-half-full kind of guy. I agree wholeheartedly with the German painter and lithographer Herm Albright, who said, "A positive attitude may not solve all your problems, but it will annoy enough people to make it worth the effort."

But even the late great Louis Armstrong, the man who made "What a Wonderful World" famous, faced tough times. Famous for his smile and ebullient attitude, he not only suffered discrimination as an African American performer in a country and industry divided by segregation and discrimination; he also endured criticism for playing in front of segregated audiences and for not being more vocal and active in the civil rights movement.

Even if you are a generally positive person, you probably also have times when you get discouraged. You may even sometimes get to the point where you wonder, "Why am I doing this?" or "What's the point?" or "Am I the only one who's not in denial?"

You may be a student who's facing a whole lot of classes you don't want to take in order to get a degree you're not sure you can use. You may be an employee who's tired of getting up every Monday, exhausting yourself through Friday, frantically trying to catch up on Saturday and Sunday, only to get up on Monday and start the whole thing all over again. Or you may be a parent whose kids don't appreciate all your sacrifices and never will until they grow up and have kids who don't appreciate *them*, and on and on it goes. Or you may be a teacher, or a public servant, or a pastor or volunteer in the church who has given so much for so long, and yet it never seems to be enough—everyone still demands more, the task is never finished.

Unless you are one of those fortunate few who never experiences disappointment or faces discouragement, whose road is always smooth and strewn with daisies and rainbows, I believe God has something to say to you through this book and through one of the most neglected parts of the whole Bible.

An Unvarnished View of Life

The ancient book of Ecclesiastes is found right near the middle of the Bible, right after the Psalms and Proverbs, two books that get a lot more attention than Ecclesiastes. But while it may be neglected and often overlooked, it is nonetheless an important—and amazingly current—piece of writing.

Many people have the impression that followers of Jesus—you know, church people, religious folk, so to speak—are just "pie in the sky" kind of people. That is, they're out of touch with the way things really are. Unrealistic. Sheltered. Strange. The general impression is that "church folk" look at things through rose-colored glasses, and they deal in platitudes and smarmy slogans. Their church signs are syrupy (when they're not offensive). Their bumper stickers are trite (when they're not offensive). Their TV shows, their songs, and their books are idealistic and impractical (when they're not offensive).

That's what a lot of people think. And, to be fair, a lot of the time they're right.

And yet . . . right in the middle of the Bible is a book, twelve chapters, called Ecclesiastes that is starkly and unrelentingly realistic, that takes an unvarnished view of life and asks the hard questions. And it doesn't answer them *at all* the way you'd expect it to.

It begins with just a brief epigraph, a few words of introduction, in verse 1, which I mentioned in Chapter One of this book:

> The words of the Teacher, son of David, king in
> Jerusalem."[14]

In other words, the pages that follow are attributed to Solomon, the son of and successor to King David. In addition to being king in Jerusalem, Solomon was also widely renowned for his wisdom and wealth. And that first verse of Ecclesiastes refers to him with a Hebrew word, *Qoheleth*, which some versions translate as "teacher," though other translations render the word as "preacher," "spokesman,"[15] "Quester,"[16] and "Philosopher."[17] There is no one word in the English language that will adequately translate *Qoheleth*, and it may even have been a proper noun, a name by which Solomon was known, perhaps like George Washington, who was called "the father of his country," or Margaret Thatcher, "The Iron Lady" who served as prime minister of England in the 1980s. In any case, *Qoheleth* was certainly meant to indicate the writer's wisdom and authority.

Depending on what version of the Bible you read from, you might see that the first eleven verses of *Qoheleth*'s book are written in the form of a poem or a song, after which, in verse 12, he begins the systematic explanation of his search, which was a quest for the meaning of life. And verse 2 actually summarizes what he concluded. He says:

> "Meaningless! Meaningless!"
>   says the Teacher.
> "Utterly meaningless!
>   Everything is meaningless."[18]

Wow. Not the most auspicious way to begin a book, is it? I mean, why don't you tell us how you really feel, *Qoheleth*? Ever think of cutting back on your caffeine intake? Ever heard of something called Prozac?

For my taste, I would much rather have him start out a little more like Norman Vincent Peale's approach in *The Power of Positive Thinking*:

> Believe in yourself! Have faith in your abilities! Without
> a humble but reasonable confidence in your own powers
> you cannot be successful or happy.[19]

Or he might have taken the tack Napoleon Hill did in his famous book *Think and Grow Rich*:

> Truly, "thoughts are things," and powerful things at that,
> when they are mixed with definiteness of purpose, persis-
> tence, and a BURNING DESIRE for their translation into
> riches, or other material objects.[20]

Or he could have chosen a punchy opening like Dr. Wayne D. Dyer's lead in *Pulling Your Own Strings*:

> You need never be a victim again. Ever![21]

That's how you start a book, right? Full of power and promise, proposing a possible change in the reader for the investment of money, time, and attention in reading your book (even if you *do* call it *Life Stinks . . . and Then You Die*).

But no. Not this guy. He starts his treatise on the meaning of life by pronouncing everything meaningless. And those ten words set the pace and establish the tone for the rest of the book. That harsh beginning shows what it's going to be like if you keep reading: you're going to get brutal honesty, stark realism, unvarnished truth. You are in for a raw confrontation with the facts of life, as seen by Solomon.

Something Pointless This Way Comes

Have you ever gotten up in the morning and asked yourself, "What am I doing? I get out of bed, I eat my Lucky Charms, I brush my teeth, I try to get my hair to do what it's supposed to do and it never does because I'm cursed. I understand all that. But what am I doing here? What's it all for? Why do I even bother?"

Maybe you've never done that. Maybe you never feel that way. But if you do, Solomon's cheerful answer to your questions is: "It all amounts to nothing. It is meaningless. Utterly meaningless. Everything is meaningless."

Now aren't you glad you picked up this book?

It's not a real jolly message, is it? But there it is. At least it puts the reader on notice: this guy isn't going to gloss over anything. He is not just blowing smoke. He is going to tell it like it is.

The word "meaningless" will appear thirty-eight times in Ecclesiastes. The old-timey (but poetic) King James Version translated it as "vanity." Other translations say "perfectly pointless"[22] or "nonsense,"[23] "useless,"[24] "futility,"[25] and "smoke, nothing but smoke."[26] The word means, literally, "breath," "vapor," or "breeze." The word denotes something passing, something empty, something that fails to satisfy.

The earliest chapters of the Bible record the story of Abel, the son of Adam and Eve.[27] Abel was a shepherd, and his brother Cain was a farmer. They both offered sacrifices to God, but Abel offered the best from his flock, while Cain "brought *some* of the fruits of the soil as an offering to the LORD."[28] God accepted Abel's offering but rejected his brother's sacrifice, which enraged Cain. So sometime later, Cain ambushed his brother and killed him. Cain became the world's first murderer, and Abel became the first murder victim.

What does that ancient story have to do with *Qoheleth*'s words? Abel's name is the same word *Qoheleth* uses in Ecclesiastes 1:2. His shortened life and senseless death point to *Qoheleth*'s verdict: meaningless. Abel's murder accomplished—nothing. It didn't assuage Cain's jealousy. It didn't solve a single problem but only created new ones. In fact, it caused separation from God and a life of exile from his family. It made nothing better; it made everything worse. Meaningless. Empty. Pointless.

That, *Qoheleth* says, is his heavily researched and well-reasoned perspective on life, and he gives four examples to support his case.

Accept That Nothing Changes

First, *Qoheleth* makes his thesis statement: everything is meaningless. Then he offers support for his statement, saying:

> What do people gain from all their labors
> at which they toil under the sun?
> Generations come and generations go,
> but the earth remains forever.
> The sun rises and the sun sets,
> and hurries back to where it rises.
> The wind blows to the south
> and turns to the north;
> round and round it goes,

ever returning on its course.
All streams flow into the sea,
　　yet the sea is never full.
To the place the streams come from,
　　there they return again.[29]

Every generation thinks it is so significant and so important. TV anchorman Tom Brokaw coined the term "The Greatest Generation" to describe the generation of people who weathered the Great Depression and fought World War II. He calls it "the greatest generation any society has ever produced."[30] He may well be right. After all, that generation defeated tyranny.

But guess what? Tyranny is back.

The Baby Boomer generation, my generation, said,

We are stardust,
we are golden,
and we've got to get ourselves back to the Garden.[31]

But guess what? The garden got crowded, everybody smelled funny, and most of us figured out we had to go home and get a job.

And sorry as I am to break it to you, today's young people are bright and beautiful and talented and energetic, but according to Solomon, they are, like all who have gone before, fodder for the perpetual, pitiless machine of life.

The earth is like an exercise bike. One generation jumps on the bike and pedals like mad until they die and fall off. And then the next generation gets on. And that generation says, "You didn't get anywhere, but we'll pedal harder."

Ecclesiastes says: Not so much. Nothing changes. He completely undercuts Couéism.

Whowhatism? you say.

Couéism.

Emile Coué was a French pharmacist who introduced a method of psychotherapy characterized by frequent repetition of the formula, "Every day, and in every way, I am becoming better and better"—a technique most famously applied by Inspector Clouseau in the *Pink Panther* films.

But *Qoheleth* says to Monsieur Coué: Not so much. Nothing really changes. Not in this life. Not "under the sun." He says, "Life isn't forward, linear progression. Life is a circle."

You say: "Things are getting better, every day, in every way."

He says, with the prophet Joni: "We're captive on a carousel of time."[32]

You say: "We're moving, we're driving, we're going places."

He says, "No, you're driving around a cul-de-sac. You're not going anywhere. Nothing really changes."

Understand That Nothing Satisfies

In verse 8 of his first chapter, *Qoheleth* adds to his case:

> All things are wearisome,
>   more than one can say.
> The eye never has enough of seeing,
>   nor the ear its fill of hearing.[33]

Sometimes when I'm reading Ecclesiastes I have to stop for a moment and pinch myself. I find myself thinking, "This is really in the Bible!"

But strange as these words sound—they are a far cry from "The Lord is my shepherd" and "Blessed are the peacemakers"—they do have the ring of truth. I mean, you wash the dishes, you have a sense of accomplishment. You walk out of the room, then back into the room; what's in the sink? The dish demon came. There are more dishes.

You get a haircut. It looks good for the rest of the day. Then you get up the next morning, and it's all jacked up. It never looks good until the next time you get it done.

You pay the bills. Good. You're done. Next day what's in the mailbox? More bills.

You go out for Chinese food. You eat so much you have to loosen your belt. You pay your bill, leave a tip, exit the restaurant. Guess what? You're hungry before you even fasten your seatbelt for the drive home.

It never ends. It's never enough. Nothing satisfies.

Recognize That Nothing Is New

Hard though it may be to believe, Solomon is just warming up. He also says, from his perspective:

> What has been will be again,
>> what has been done will be done again;
>> there is nothing new under the sun.
> Is there anything of which one can say,
>> "Look! This is something new"?
> It was here already, long ago;
>> it was here before our time.[34]

Nothing new under the sun?

Come on, Solomon, what about airplanes? He'd say, "What about birds?"

Okay, what about reality TV? He'd say, "Stupid people and voyeurs were around in my day, too."

Okay, but ever hear of a thing called nuclear power? He'd say, "Ever hear of a thing called Genesis 1?"

He is right. We don't have any new ideas. We take old ideas and we recycle them, and we get all excited because they're new to us.

That's why fashions get dumber and dumber. You can't have new fashion. We've tried everything from naked to muumuu. If you want to be creative today, you go to the vintage store and wear old clothes.

Even the realization that nothing is new is nothing new. Rudyard Kipling wrote:

> The craft that we call modern,
> The crimes that we call new,
> John Bunyan had 'em typed and filed
> In Sixteen Eighty-two.[35]

There is nothing new "under the sun," *Qoheleth* says. Everything has been done before; we just weren't paying attention.

Realize That Nothing Lasts

In verse 11, Solomon finally issues his grand finale, the culmination of his opening argument:

> No one remembers the former generations,
> and even those yet to come
> will not be remembered
> by those who follow.[36]

Let me conduct a quick survey. Don't worry, it's harmless. No salesman will call, and your credit card won't be charged. In fact, chances are, it will be over for you by the second round. Ready?

Here is the first question: what are your parents' names?

Very good. Now for round two: what are the names of your four grandparents?

How did you do? Let's go on to round three: can you name one of your great-grandparents? What about great-great-grandparents?

Solomon knew what he was talking about. Even with the wonders of the Internet and such amazing resources as Ancestry.com:

No one remembers the former generations,
> and even those yet to come
will not be remembered
> by those who follow.

Solomon says, "Nothing lasts." Bridges collapse. Levees fail. Friends betray. People forget.

So by now you're thinking, *man, this is depressing.* Right? It is really depressing, but it is also brutally honest. And it is heading to a point.

Once Solomon sings his depressing theme song, he changes from poetry to prose without changing his tune.

Beyond Cockeyed Optimism

After hitting us over the head with a two-by-four in the first eleven verses of his book, Solomon goes on to give us a little background for his sweeping pronouncements:

> I, the Teacher, was king over Israel in Jerusalem. I applied my mind to study and to explore by wisdom all that is done under the heavens. What a heavy burden God has laid on mankind! I have seen all the things that are done under the sun; all of them are meaningless, a chasing after the wind.

> What is twisted cannot be straightened;
> > what is lacking cannot be counted.

> I thought to myself, "Look, I have grown and increased in wisdom more than anyone who has ruled over Jerusalem before me; I have experienced much of wisdom and knowledge." Then I applied myself to the understanding of wisdom, and also of madness and folly, but I learned that this, too, is a chasing after the wind.

> For with much wisdom comes much sorrow;
> the more knowledge, the more grief.[37]

In other words, he says, "Listen, I'm a king. I've used my wealth and wisdom and experience to try it all, to try to find answers. I've done my homework, and all I've learned has only made me sadder."

So . . . are you glad you picked up this book? Not yet?

Seriously, I wouldn't blame you if you are feeling a tad glum right now. At least we know Solomon's not going to tell us something just to make us feel better. So there are several ways we can respond to Solomon's blunt assessment.

The first: we can dismiss it. We can shrug it off. Ignore it. Pretend it doesn't exist. We can follow Maria's advice in *The Sound of Music* and just try thinking of our favorite things, and maybe then we won't feel so bad. Or we can emulate Anna in *The King and I* by striking a careless pose as we "whistle a happy tune." Or like Nellie in *South Pacific*, we could be "cockeyed optimists" and just "forget every cloud I've ever seen." Or we could do all three; we could call it the "Hollywood Musical Cure for the Blues." Maybe we could even market it on late-night infomercials.

That's one way we can respond to Solomon's blunt assessment. But there are other ways that are far better than denial and cockeyed optimism, ways that will give us a good start toward living well in a sick world. Let me suggest just a few, in the light of Ecclesiastes 1.

Strive to Live Your Life with Brutal Honesty

Denial is nobody's friend. I believe Ecclesiastes is in the Bible partly because God wants you to know that it is okay to be realistic. It is not unbiblical to say, "Life stinks." It is not unspiritual to say, "Life's not fair." It is not unchristian to say, like James, "this should not be."[38] Contrary to popular belief, faith is not denying the obvious; faith is seeing things as they truly are, while simultaneously seeing *beyond* things as they truly are.

Trust God with What He Already Knows

Too often, when life stinks, we think we have to protect God—or his reputation—from damage. But he knows the true state of things better than we do and, as Philip Yancey says, "we must trust God with what God already knows."[39] One lesson Solomon teaches us is that God is big enough to hear what we really feel, what we really think . . . whether it's a mid-life crisis or bitterness over an unanswered prayer or unrealized dream, or grief from a loss, or guilt over a sin, or anger over injustice, or impatience or frustration or confusion or whatever. You can be sure that God is aware of things as they really are, and you can always trust him with what he already knows. So don't pretend. Don't pray platitudes. Don't be afraid to acknowledge what is real or feel what you are truly feeling.

Don't Be Fooled by Anything "Under the Sun"

Solomon tells us, right up front, "I have seen all the things that are done under the sun; all of them are meaningless, a chasing after the wind."[40] The phrase "under the sun" is key.

Charles Swindoll says that *Qoheleth*'s perspective is the same viewpoint most people operate from today:

> It is an "under-the-sun" perspective. Time after time, Solomon mentions his horizontal, strictly human viewpoint. In virtually every major section of his journal he uses the words "under the sun" and "under heaven." . . . Because he seldom looks "above the sun" to find reassurance, life seems drab and depressing, hopelessly meaningless. In spite of the extent to which he went to find happiness, because he left God out of the picture, nothing

satisfied. It never will. Satisfaction in life under the sun
will never occur until there is a meaningful connection
with the living Lord above the sun.[41]

This earth and this life are great and gracious gifts, but if we are
looking for satisfaction and fulfillment from earthly comforts and
momentary pleasures, we may expect to be woefully disappointed.
We have much to be grateful for here and now but nothing to be satisfied with. It is a paradox expressed well in the song by Caedmon's
Call, "This World":

> This world has nothing for me
> And this world has everything;
> All that I could want
> And nothing that I need.[42]

That is a helpful attitude toward this life and the things of this world.
And it is a key perspective to keep in mind as you discover more of
Solomon's wisdom in the book of Ecclesiastes.

————— ⤳ —————

*A*bba, Father, I don't want to succumb to either cynicism or cockeyed optimism. I don't want to live in denial. I want to see the things of this life clearly. I want to have the right attitudes toward this life, so I pray that you'll teach me those right attitudes through this book. Help me to live my life with brutal honesty; give me the faith that sees things as they truly are, while simultaneously seeing beyond things as they truly are.

Help me to trust you with what I really feel and think, whether it's a mid-life crisis, bitterness over an unanswered prayer or unrealized dream, grief from a loss, guilt from sin, anger over injustice, impatience, frustration, confusion, whatever. Help me not to pretend. Help me not to pray platitudes. Help me to acknowledge what is real in me and submit it to the ultimate, infinite reality that is in you.

And, Father, help me not to be fooled by anything "under the sun," not to look for satisfaction and fulfillment in earthly comforts and momentary pleasures, but to ever and always look to you to meet my needs and fulfill my hopes. In Jesus' name, amen.

chapter THREE

THE FASTER I GO, THE BEHINDER I GET

I received an email yesterday from an editor. He's efficient. Thorough. Extremely detail oriented (as most editors tend to be; it's part of the editor's basic tool kit).

But the email wasn't addressed to me. In fact, it was *about* me.

Happily, the email wasn't critical of me. It didn't list my faults or detail my shortcomings. Quite the contrary, in fact. The editor had addressed the email to a financial person in his publishing company, pointing out a small inconsistency in the contract they had signed with me. A financial inconsistency. And the editor was requesting that the company pay me more than both he and I had agreed on, based on that inconsistency and because, he wrote, "he earned it with all he did, and he was even remarkably on time (actually early on all his turn-in dates)."

I wasn't supposed to see that email. Three hours later, I received another email in which the editor confessed his mistake, adding,

"That's what happens when you go too fast and are trying to get too many things done."

Don't I know it.

You probably do, too. Who hasn't wished there was some way to call back an email just seconds after pressing "Send"? Who hasn't tried to do too many things at once? Who hasn't regretted moving faster and faster while slipping further and further behind?

That's one of the reasons life stinks. Just a few generations ago, the pace of human life was defined by the turning of the seasons, the phases of the moon:

seedtime and harvest,
cold and heat,
summer and winter,
day and night.[43]

But those days are gone. We live in an on-the-go, hurry-up, drive-thru world. Our modern world seems to spin much faster than ever before, a world "in which mothers work, stores don't close, assembly lines never stop, TV beckons all the time, and stock traders have to keep up with the action in Tokyo."[44] There are so many demands on our time, and they come, like Hamlet's sorrows, "not as single spies, but in battalions."[45] Long work hours, demanding school schedules, parenting responsibilities, social media, the increasing demands of bureaucracy (taxes, insurance, record-keeping), and the twenty-four-hour news cycle conspire against us. Even if time were to slow down for a few moments, we would pass it right on by; we have forgotten how to slow down—if we ever knew.

A recent study of pedestrians in more than thirty cities around the world reveals that even our walking is faster than ever before. The average pedestrian attained a speed of 3.5 miles per hour—10 percent faster than just ten years earlier! Psychologist Richard

Wiseman, who compiled the research and published it in a book entitled *Quirkology*, suggests, "The bottom line is that the pace of life is now ten percent faster."[46]

And it is getting faster all the time. We are only half joking when we tell a co-worker, "I need it yesterday." In many cases, we need it even sooner than that.

Faster Than the Speed of Life

It seems ridiculous to expect answers to our modern frenzy in a 3,000-year-old book that is attributed to a man who had unfathomable wealth and countless slaves at his beck and call. What could an absolute monarch who ruled over an Iron-Age Middle Eastern kingdom possibly have to teach us about life in the hectic, hurried twenty-first century? Can the ancient book of Ecclesiastes possibly be of any help to men and women whose lives resemble a NASCAR time trial more than anything else?

You'd be surprised.

King Solomon was not a layabout. He may have lived in a slower, less technologically advanced time than you and I do, but he seems to have kept a pretty demanding schedule. Judging from the first chapters of 2 Chronicles in the Bible, he:

- acquired 1,400 chariots
- imported, bought, or bred 12,000 horses
- exported horses and chariots to other nations
- established "chariot cities" throughout his kingdom
- designed, built, furnished, and staffed the Temple of God, one of the wonders of the ancient world
- designed, built, and furnished a new royal palace in Jerusalem
- rebuilt and settled villages annexed from Hiram, king of Tyre

- conquered and captured Hamath Zobah in Syria
- rebuilt Tadmor, Upper Beth Horon, Lower Beth Horon, Baalath, and numerous other cities as store cities and fortified cities
- conscripted slave laborers from among Israel's enemies
- recruited, trained, and administered hundreds of court officials
- established a robust economy of tribute from other kings and nations
- commissioned the manufacture of hundreds of hammered gold shields, an elaborate throne room, golden goblets, and other household articles
- commissioned a merchant navy
- established and defended sophisticated supply routes
- established key alliances with neighboring nations
- married and maintained 700 wives
- acquired and maintained a harem of 300 concubines
- entertained the rich and powerful, such as the Queen of Sheba
- composed 3,000 proverbs
- wrote more than a thousand songs
- produced manuals on botany and biology
- wrote (or is credited with writing) three books of the Bible (Proverbs, Ecclesiastes, Song of Solomon)

And that is a partial list! (For example, with all his wives and concubines, he probably fathered numerous children, though the Bible only mentions three—two daughters and a son). And though some of his accomplishments are definitely not exemplary, they do indicate a man who had more than a few things to keep him busy. Keep in mind, too, that he accomplished all that in an age before online shopping was a possibility. However he selected his 700 wives and 300 concubines, he never availed himself of eHarmony.com or similar services. And all his building projects were furnished and outfitted without resorting to IKEA or Bed Bath & Beyond.

So maybe King Solomon does have something to offer. Perhaps *Qoheleth*'s book applies far more to us than a casual glance might suggest. I think so. In fact, I think the second chapter of Ecclesiastes actually contains four timely pointers for living wisely and well in a world that is moving faster than the speed of life.

Don't Pursue Pleasure and Prosperity

Why are we so busy? Why are we so pressed for time? Why do we go so fast trying to get so much done? Why are we moving faster and faster while slipping further and further behind?

So many of life's tasks that used to be hard and time-consuming are now relatively easy and quick. I can load the dishwasher in a fraction of the time it used to take to fill the sink, wash, rinse, and dry a day's worth of dishes. If we're running low on groceries, I can drive to the store in minutes and be home before the oven is done preheating. I can research something on the Internet in nanoseconds compared to just a couple decades ago, when I might have driven to the library, searched numerous reference texts, made notes, and probably still had to wait for interlibrary loans to complete the task.

But I'm more pressed for time than ever. Why? What has happened? Solomon points us to an answer:

> I said to myself, "Come now, I will test you with pleasure to find out what is good." But that also proved to be meaningless. "Laughter," I said, "is madness. And what does pleasure accomplish?" I tried cheering myself with wine, and embracing folly—my mind still guiding me with wisdom. I wanted to see what was worthwhile for people to do under the heavens during the few days of their lives.

I undertook great projects: I built houses for myself
and planted vineyards. I made gardens and parks and
planted all kinds of fruit trees in them. I made reservoirs
to water groves of flourishing trees. I bought male and
female slaves and had other slaves who were born in my
house. I also owned more herds and flocks than anyone in
Jerusalem before me. I amassed silver and gold for myself,
and the treasure of kings and provinces. I acquired male
and female singers, and a harem as well—the delights
of a man's heart. I became greater by far than anyone in
Jerusalem before me. In all this my wisdom stayed with me.

> I denied myself nothing my eyes desired;
>   I refused my heart no pleasure.
> My heart took delight in all my labor,
>   and this was the reward for all my toil.
> Yet when I surveyed all that my hands had done
>   and what I had toiled to achieve,
> everything was meaningless, a chasing after the wind;
>   nothing was gained under the sun.[47]

The wise *Qoheleth* describes the pursuit of two things that led him
nowhere. First was the pursuit of pleasure—leisure and laughter,
cheer and amusement. In his ancient milieu, that meant experiment-
ing with wine and testing various forms of folly. If he were conducting
the same exercise today, the possibilities would have seemed endless:
180 cable TV channels, pay-per-view, Netflix, YouTube, Facebook,
Twitter, Pinterest, *Monday Night Football*, March Madness, the
latest 3D movie, immersive video game experiences, karaoke at
the neighborhood bar, concerts, comedy clubs, museums, parties,
paintball courses, keno and casinos, and on and on it goes. Modern

life is saturated with entertainment options. There are more ways to entertain ourselves than ever before in human history.

For example, children's parties are big business now. Birthday parties for all ages, bar mitzvahs and bat mitzvahs, and quinceañera (fifteenth) and "sweet sixteen" parties have become major events in many families. Some parents hire party planners for such events and spend tens of thousands of dollars. Party planner Leesa Zelken says:

> Twenty years ago a clown making balloon animals was a big deal, princess playing games with children was a huge attraction and drew a lot of oohs and ahhs from people.... Over time that's become run of the mill. Now people are trying to not only outdo one another but trying to outdo themselves.[48]

And it is getting worse: the average dollar amount spent on entertainment on such events recently increased 29 percent in just one year.[49]

Regardless of your age (or your children's ages), chances are that part of your busyness today is due to entertainments and pleasures that were not available to you just a decade or two ago—whether because of advancing technology, greater affluence, or the availability of exponentially more options. A few years ago, I was pastoring a growing church, trying to meet book deadlines, and trying to find time to enjoy my first grandchildren. Something had to give. I was constantly pressed and stressed for time. My life wasn't working. Things came to a head one Saturday when I realized that the two college football teams I followed most closely had back-to-back televised games. That meant I *needed* to move things around in my schedule to make room for six hours or more of football. It was a crisis, especially since my hometown NFL team's game would be televised the next afternoon, after church. Suddenly I had a revelation. It was horrifying in its clarity. It's not for everyone, I grant, but

I realized that I did not have to watch those football games. In fact, I somehow understood that pursuing the pleasure of six or more hours of televised football on most weekends was more than a little excessive, considering how many time pressures I had to juggle in any given week. I was making my life more difficult by pursuing that harmless pleasure. So I quit. Cold turkey. I not only gave up televised football, I decided then and there that I had other priorities that trumped all televised sports events (unless, of course, the Cincinnati Reds made the playoffs; after all, I'm not Amish).

I'm not suggesting that course of action for everyone. And we all need a hobby or a good laugh from time to time (after all, one of the proverbs Solomon himself collected says, "A cheerful heart is good medicine"[50]). But with the explosion of entertainment and leisure options in recent decades, many of us have unthinkingly added to our expectations. We *have to* see that movie. We *have to* use those tickets. We *have to* give our kid a cool birthday party. We *have to* do all sorts of pleasurable things that we don't really *have to* do. *The Message* paraphrases *Qoheleth*'s conclusion regarding pleasure like this: "My verdict on the pursuit of happiness? Who needs it?"[51]

But it's not just pleasure that runs us around in circles; the pursuit of prosperity does, too. *Qoheleth* describes the building of houses, planting of vineyards, and the designing of gardens, parks, pools, and orchards. He details the accumulation of wealth in slaves, gold, silver, and court musicians. Each year was better than the last. Every project bigger than the one before. He would have fit right in with us today.

A curious thing has happened over the course of our lifetimes. Somewhere along the line we started working harder and longer to pursue a standard of living King Solomon himself would have called "greater by far than anyone . . . before." For example, the typical size of a single-family home built in 1950 was less than a thousand square feet.[52] In 2011, the average single-family house completed was 2,480 square feet,[53] and homes of 4,000–10,000 square feet are becoming more common than ever. The trend is not only outward but upward as well: in the 1980s, less than 15 percent of new homes in the U.S. had nine-foot ceilings; that percentage has tripled in the twenty-first century.

Even in times of recession and hardship, our economic expectations are several times removed from what we would have considered normal just one or two generations ago. Consider the following comparison between the norms of my upbringing and those of my grandchildren:

	Bob	Bob's grandkids
motto	"Use it up, wear it out, make it do or do without"	"Bigger/better/faster"
cars in garage	1 (no garage, mom rode bus to work)	2
telephones	kitchen, upstairs extension	adults/teens all have smartphones
televisions	one 19" black-and-white Zenith	2 or 3 large-screen HDTVs
computers	none	desktop, laptop, iPad, LeapPad, etc.
air conditioning	window fans	central air conditioner
appliances	refrigerator/freezer, oven/range, clothes washer only	refrigerator/freezer/icemaker, oven/range, washer/dryer, dishwasher, microwave, disposal
eating out	Sunday smorgasbord once a month	several times a week
vacation trips	none, other than trips to visit relatives	regular

There's nothing wrong with any of that, of course. Part of "The American Dream" is that our children and grandchildren will have it better than we did, right? Right.

But building bigger and bigger houses, acquiring more and more, and becoming "greater by far" in possessions than our parents and grandparents comes at a price. We must earn more and work more in order to afford more. And maintain it. And insure it. And life becomes more demanding. Psychologist Tim Kasser of Knox College says, "The more people focus on a materialistic pathway to happiness, the less happy they tend to be."[54]

Frederick Charles Jennings, a teacher and author among the Plymouth Brethren in the early twentieth century, was right when he wrote,

> Accumulation brings with it only disappointment and added care,—everything is permeated with a common poison; and here the wisdom of the old is, in one sense, in full harmony with the higher wisdom of the new, which says "godliness, with contentment, is great gain," and "having food and raiment, let us be therewith content."[55]

Don't Look to Learning for Fulfillment

Suddenly, the ancient *Qoheleth* begins to make modern sense. If he is right that our pursuit of pleasure and prosperity is partly responsible for our frustrating lives, maybe he is right about other things as well—such as the value of learning and education in finding the fulfillment our hearts seek. Beginning in Ecclesiastes 2:12, he writes:

> Then I turned my thoughts to consider wisdom,
>   and also madness and folly.
> What more can the king's successor do
>   than what has already been done?
> I saw that wisdom is better than folly,
>   just as light is better than darkness.
> The wise man have eyes in their heads,
>   while the fool walks in the darkness;
> but I came to realize
>   that the same fate overtakes them both.

Then I thought in my heart,

"The fate of the fool will overtake me also.
    What then do I gain by being wise?"
I said in my heart,
    "This too is meaningless."
For the wise man, like the fool, will not be long
remembered;
    the days have already come when both have been
    forgotten.
Like the fool, the wise man too must die![56]

Qoheleth is not saying that education has no value; on the contrary, he says that wisdom is better than folly. Learning is better than ignorance. Education is better than stagnation. I am a great believer in education, despite having squeezed four years of high school into five and having taken fourteen years to finish undergraduate studies. There are so many books yet to read, classes to take, languages to learn, skills to acquire, that I can't possibly find the time to die until I'm well into my 120s. I haven't stopped learning yet, and I don't plan to.

But education is a means, not an end. *Qoheleth* identifies three limitations of education.

1. It is not transferable. "What more can the king's successor do than what has already been done?"[57] he asks. Quite possibly, *Qoheleth* had become the most learned man on the face of the earth in his time, accomplished in science, literature, politics, architecture, and more. Yet he could not transplant that education into his son; he could not transfer his wisdom to his heirs. His educational accomplishments could not ensure that his successor would live well or rule wisely (in fact, the Bible records the folly of King Solomon's son and successor in 2 Chronicles 10).

2. It does not guarantee harmony, health, or happiness. "The wise have eyes in their heads," *Qoheleth* wrote, "while the fool walks in the darkness; but I came to realize that the same fate overtakes them both."[58]

There are advantages to education, of course, but educated people lose their jobs, spoil their kids, mess up their marriages, drive their businesses into the ground, and eventually die, just like uneducated people. It is folly to think otherwise. The British journalist and satirist Malcolm Muggeridge wrote:

> Education—the great mumbo jumbo and fraud of the ages—purports to equip us to live and is prescribed as a universal remedy for everything from juvenile delinquency to premature senility.
>
> For the most part it serves to enlarge stupidity, inflate conceit, enhance credulity, and put those subjected to it at the mercy of brainwashers with printing presses, radio, and television at their disposal.[59]

If education were the answer, college campuses would be utopias of harmony, health, and happiness. If learning were the path to fulfillment and purpose in life, university professors and presidents would be the happiest people on earth. But they are not. Believe me. As a pastor in a college town for more than ten years, I've known more than my share, counted many as good friends, and counseled quite a few. And I can testify that *Qoheleth*'s ancient conclusion is supported by my contemporary experience: the highly educated experience the same disappointments and dysfunctions as the uneducated (most, however, can describe their problems in bigger words!).

3. It is an insufficient legacy. Michael Nicholson is a resident of Kalamazoo, Michigan. According to an article in the New York Daily News, Nicholson earned his first college degree in 1963, a bachelor's in religious education from William Tyndale College in Michigan. Since then, he has obtained twenty-eight other degrees—including twenty-two master's degrees and a doctorate—in fields as diverse as educational leadership, library science, home economics, health education, and law enforcement. He hopes to live long enough (he is currently in his early seventies) to finish his thirty-third or thirty-fourth degree around the time he reaches eighty or eighty-one years old. At that point, he says, "I'll feel like I've completed my basic education." Nicholson may well be the most educated person on the planet (his wife, who helps him with his homework, has earned seven degrees of her own!), and his lifelong habit of learning is commendable and inspiring. But someday, his educational accomplishments will be listed in a fascinating obituary. They may even be listed on his tombstone. But even the most educated person in the world will not always be remembered; in *Qoheleth*'s words, the day will come when the wise and the fool alike will be forgotten.

None of these are reasons to reject education. *Qoheleth* is not saying—nor am I—that we should stop learning. But education is ultimately unsatisfying. It is not sufficient. It can never fulfill the deepest and best longings of the human heart.

Don't Lose Yourself in Work

As a pastor for many years in a college town, I've seen it happen over and over again. Some of the best students in the nation compete for the top spots in business. Many of them enter the workforce at a level of pay and benefits that boggles the mind—at least, it boggles mine! Just a few short months after graduation, they've grabbed hold of the ladder of success and begun climbing. They work hard. They work long. They sacrifice for the company. They get promoted. They take on more responsibility. They earn raises. They win awards and recognition.

And then something happens. It is almost as predictable as sunrise and sunset. They wake up one day and wonder what happened. Where did the time go? How did they miss so many of their kids' ball games and school concerts? When did they become strangers to their spouses? What happened to their youthful idealism, all their previous plans and priorities? In a few words: they lost themselves in their work.

Qoheleth says the same thing happened to him, in Ecclesiastes 2:17–23:

> So I hated life, because the work that is done under the
> sun was grievous to me. All of it is meaningless, a chasing
> after the wind. I hated all the things I had toiled for under
> the sun, because I must leave them to the one who comes
> after me. And who knows whether that person will be
> wise or foolish? Yet they will have control over all the fruit
> of my toil into which I have poured my effort and skill
> under the sun. This too is meaningless. So my heart began
> to despair over all my toilsome labor under the sun. For a
> person may labor with wisdom, knowledge and skill, and
> then they must leave all they own to another who has not
> toiled for it. This too is meaningless and a great misfor-
> tune. What do people get for all the toil and anxious striv-
> ing with which they labor under the sun? All their days
> their work is grief and pain; even at night their minds do
> not rest. This too is meaningless.[60]

Qoheleth discovered how meaningless it is to lose yourself in your work. If anyone on earth could have found satisfaction and fulfillment in his life's work, you'd think it would have been Solomon, the builder of the Jerusalem Temple, one of the wonders of the ancient world. But his life experimentation and exploration taught him three fundamental things.

1. You are not what you do. How many times has someone greeted you at some social function with the question, "So . . . what do you do?" After exchanging names, it is often the first piece of information we share with new acquaintances. We may have recently completed a marathon, lost twenty pounds, or learned to play the tuba, but those things won't be mentioned, because we live in a culture that tends to define people by their job or career—or lack thereof. But *Qoheleth* describes his work as, "grievous . . . meaningless, a chasing after the wind."[61] It did not define him, and it shouldn't define you. If you allow your work to define you, then what happens when you lose your job? When you change careers? When you retire? Such changes come in the course of a lifetime—and even more so in difficult times; if your identity is wrapped up in what you do, you will probably face repeated (and distressing) identity crises. But if you are a child of God, a follower of Jesus—chosen, royal, priestly, holy[62]—then your identity is not based on some role or function "under the sun," but on something far more lasting, solid, and substantial.

2. You are not indispensable. A dozen years ago, my wife and I helped to plant a church in the college town to which I've already referred a time or two. As the only ordained member of the small group of friends that started the church, I served that flock as a pastor—first as a volunteer for five years, then as part of the paid staff. After eleven years of pouring heart and soul into that church, I passed the baton to other leaders—and was soon disappointed and offended that the church continued to function well without my expertise! As a matter of fact, all four of the churches I served as pastor over the years managed to keep on going and growing after my departure. But so it goes. Whether you're a king or a college president, a pastor or a pastry chef, you will someday find out (if you haven't already) that you are not indispensable. Like *Qoheleth*, who complained that someone else would eventually "have control over all the fruit of my toil into which I have poured my effort and skill under the sun,"[63] you will look back and see that all your stress and struggle—as if you were indispensable—amounted to nothing. You will see how much healthier, wiser, and more effective it would have been to work hard and well without losing yourself in the job.

3. You can't take it with you. We lose ourselves in work for many reasons. We want to make Dad or Mom—or husband or wife— proud. We feel a sense of responsibility to the company. We're gunning for a position that will make many of our financial dreams come true. We want to prove our worth to someone. We want our kids to have a lifestyle we never had. We want to retire early. And so on.

But whatever it is that drives you to work too hard, stress too much, and slave too long, you will find it ultimately unsatisfying— and utterly unsustainable. Like King Solomon, you will find sooner or later that all you worked so hard for will belong to someone else— whether your goal was approval, recognition, wealth, or something else. Even the satisfaction of accomplishment itself is fleeting. As Henry Ward Beecher said, "Success is full of promise until men get it, and then it is last year's nest from which the birds have flown."[64]

Solomon had to confront the reality that the fruits of all his hard work would, in the end, be passed on to another—in his case, his son and heir, Rehoboam. Interestingly, the Bible reveals nothing about Rehoboam until it tells us that Solomon died and his son Rehoboam succeeded him. Nothing about his birth. Nothing of his life. Nothing until he took his father's royal position and proceeded so unwisely that the kingdom split and many of his subjects rebelled against him, fulfilling *Qoheleth*'s lament:

I hated all the things I had toiled for under the sun, because
I must leave them to the one who comes after me. And
who knows whether that person will be wise or foolish? Yet
they will have control over all the fruit of my toil into which
I have poured my effort and skill under the sun. . . . For a
person may labor with wisdom, knowledge and skill, and
then they must leave all they own to another who has not
toiled for it. This too is meaningless and a great misfortune.[65]

Please God

For all *Qoheleth*'s brutal, blunt honesty, Ecclesiastes 2 is not all gloom
and doom. Like the rest of the book, it is not only about how "life
stinks," but also about how to live well in a sick world. Thus, it ends
with the first of six "conclusions" *Qoheleth* offers to anyone with the
intestinal fortitude to keep reading. While the pages of Ecclesiastes
detail and often repeat the futility of a perspective that looks no
higher than "under the sun" for wisdom, each of *Qoheleth*'s six conclusions[66] lifts the reader's gaze beyond this life and its limitations.

A person can do nothing better than to eat and drink and
find satisfaction in their own toil. This too, I see, is from
the hand of God, for without him, who can eat or find
enjoyment? To the person who pleases him, God gives
wisdom, knowledge and happiness, but to the sinner he
gives the task of gathering and storing up wealth to hand it
over to the one who pleases God. This too is meaningless,
a chasing after the wind.[67]

Qoheleth has not mentioned God once since Ecclesiastes 1:13 ("What
a heavy burden God has laid on mankind!"). His discussion of pleasure
and prosperity, education and work, has been from a gritty, earthly
perspective. But notice how the mood lifts when his outlook shifts.

After pointing out the emptiness and meaninglessness of prosperity, education, and work, *Qoheleth* says, "A person can do nothing better than to eat and drink and find satisfaction in their own toil."[68] Is he contradicting himself? Did he change his mind? Is he schizophrenic?

None of the above. He says that pursuing pleasure is not the path to pleasure. Amassing diplomas and degrees will not lead to wisdom. Losing oneself in work will not bring satisfaction. Such things as those—eating and drinking and work—can only be enjoyed when they are received from the hand of God and pursued with the intention of pleasing him.

I recently made a trip to the eye doctor. My current prescription glasses were several years old, and I had noticed some changes in my vision that suggested I needed a new prescription. I spent a little under an hour with the optometrist. During that time, he told me repeatedly, "look here" and "look there." He instructed me to read this line or that line of text. He pointed my focus one direction while asking me how many fingers he held up in another direction. When it was all over, he wrote me a new prescription and promised that I would see substantial improvement with my new pair of glasses. The results would have been quite different, however, if I had repeatedly focused my gaze someplace other than where he pointed me. It would be foolish, of course, for me to expect success if I had insisted on looking "there" when he said to look "here." He probably would have kicked me out of his office and told me not to return until I was willing to cooperate with the process.

The same is true for the man or woman who wants to live well in a sick world. It starts with the proper focus. If we are focused on pursuing pleasure or status or success, we are looking in the wrong direction. That pursuit will always disappoint us, because fulfillment doesn't come from pleasure, prosperity, education, or work; it comes from God. "[A]sk God, who gives generously to all without finding fault, and it will be given to you."[69] "[G]o after God, who piles on all the riches we could ever manage."[70] "To the person who pleases him, God gives wisdom, knowledge, and happiness. . . ."[71]

Author and educator Leonard Sweet writes in his book *Soul Salsa* of a small printed card he keeps in his wallet:

> The card has only two words on it and one grammatical marking. The card is black. The words are gold. Between the two words is an x-ed out comma. The words I keep in front of my credit cards are these:[72]

Sweet explains that his governing goal in life is to remove the comma from that phrase, transforming it from "the Mayday prayer 'Please, God' to the Good Friday prayer of 'Please God.' The removal of one little comma can change a prayer from 'What can you do for me?' to 'How can your purposes be fulfilled in my life?'"[73]

That is what we need. That is what *Qoheleth* was getting at. The soul that can remove that comma will begin to turn the corner in life. That soul will stop begging God to bless its efforts at finding pleasure and prosperity, satisfaction and fulfillment, and instead seek God's pleasure in all it does. *That* soul will experience the wisdom, knowledge, and happiness God gives to the person who pleases him.

———— ∾ ————

*ather God, I confess that I have often sought satis-
faction in pleasure and prosperity, in buying and
having and owning and enjoying things. I confess that I have
pursued fulfillment in education, expecting knowledge and
achievement to satisfy the hunger of my heart and quench
the thirsting of my soul. I confess that I have tended to lose
myself in work, accepting the lie that "who I am" is "what I
do," believing in my own indispensability, and banking on
job security and financial security more than on you, my
true and only security. I confess that these idolatrous pursuits have bred soul stress and soul sickness in my life, rather
than satisfaction and fulfillment. I repent of those things
and thank you for the forgiveness that is mine in Christ.
Help me to stop begging you to bless my efforts at finding
pleasure and prosperity, knowledge and security, but to
look to you as my soul's pleasure, my wisdom, my joy, and
my security. Teach me that godliness with contentment is a
great gain. Help me to remove that comma that was talked
about above, transforming my life prayer from "Please, God"
to "Please God." In Jesus' name, amen.*

GETTING DIZZY IN THE "CIRCLE OF LIFE"

Chris Gardner was a good guy.

Fresh out of the U.S. Navy, he moved to San Francisco to pursue a prestigious research job and an opportunity to work for one of the top heart surgeons in the country. He fell in love with the city. He worked hard. When he had a son, he wanted more than anything to provide for him.

But life dealt Chris one bad hand after another. His girlfriend left. He lost his apartment. He ended up homeless, without even a car to sleep in. Working impossible hours and against impossible odds, he spent nearly a year moving himself and his son between homeless shelters, soup kitchens, even sleeping in a metro station bathroom.

You may recognize Chris's story from the book—and the hit movie, starring Will Smith—*The Pursuit of Happyness*. It is an amazing story, and a true one, of one man's determination to rise above crushing setbacks and become a success not only as a powerful player in the world of finance, but also as a father . . . and a man.

You may never have experienced that kind of thing. Maybe your life has been just one steady climb, rung by rung, up the ladder of success. Maybe the soundtrack of your life is filled with only happy songs, songs by the Carpenters or Carrie Underwood, or maybe from "It's a Small World."

If that's the case, well, good for you. I don't think I like you very much, but good for you.

Then again, maybe that doesn't adequately describe your journey. Maybe, like most folks, you've experienced your share of ups and downs. You've had good times, sure. You've been blessed . . . and you're grateful for those blessings. But frankly, sometimes life stinks. Sometimes, like Chris Gardner, you try and try, and it seems that the deck is stacked against you, and while you've still got stuff to be thankful for, the soundtrack of *your* life could be filled with songs by Damien Rice, Sarah McLachlan, and Amy Winehouse.

Either way, it is possible to live well in this sick world. It is possible, as people from King Solomon to Chris Gardner have shown us, to face the worst circumstances without losing hope.

Stuff Happens

This ancient book of Ecclesiastes, which is attributed to King Solomon, the son of King David, a man who had tried everything—wine, women, song, money, sex, and power, you name it—in a systematic attempt to figure out life, never minces words. Some Bible readers find it too blunt. Some think it is too cynical. Some have even questioned its place in the canon of Scripture (though it is one of five Bible books known as the *Megilloth*[74] ["scrolls"], the short books that are read every year at one of the feasts in the Jewish calendar and have been accepted by the church since at least the second century[75]).

But anyone who values transparency, honesty, and real-life experience will appreciate Ecclesiastes. *Qoheleth* tells the reader right up front and repeats it over and over:

> I have seen all the things that are done under the sun; all
> of them are meaningless, a chasing after the wind.[76]

In other words, "life stinks . . . and then you die." Stuff happens. This
world is not for the faint of heart. As Pat, the character played by
Bradley Cooper in the movie *Silver Linings Playbook*, said, "This
world'll break your heart ten ways to Sunday. That's guaranteed."
This life can knock you down like a Whack-a-Mole and kick you
around like a bull does a rodeo clown (you can file that under "Great
Theological Truths").

Ecclesiastes never paints life any other way. It is gritty and
straightforward. But it also shows us conclusively that God loves the
hard questions, and he doesn't insist on pat answers. He not only
inspired *Qoheleth* to record his thoughts, but he slipped these twelve
chapters into the Bible and preserved their candor and beauty for
something like three thousand years, so that people caught in the
tornadic twenty-first century could read and learn from them.

And part of the treasure God inspired and preserved for us is
one of the most familiar passages in Scripture, the first eight verses
of Ecclesiastes 3, where the seeker after truth, the author of the book,
says this:

> There is a time for everything,
> > and a season for every activity under the heavens:
>
> a time to be born and a time to die,
> > a time to plant and a time to uproot,
> a time to kill and a time to heal,
> > a time to tear down and a time to build,
> a time to weep and a time to laugh,
> > a time to mourn and a time to dance,
> a time to scatter stones and a time to gather them,
> > a time to embrace and a time to from embracing,

> a time to search and a time to give up,
>
> > a time to keep and a time to throw away,
>
> a time to tear and a time to mend,
>
> > a time to be silent and a time to speak,
>
> a time to love and a time to hate,
>
> > a time for war and a time for peace.[77]

Some of those words are a little hard to hear, aren't they? Some are not at all "politically correct." Some seem way too harsh, too blunt, too real, for our delicate modern ears.

"A time to die"?

"A time to kill"?

"A time to hate"?

We don't want to hear that, especially those of us who have lived all our lives in the U.S. of A. (or what Len Sweet, one of my favorite authors, calls "USAmerica"). We don't have ears to hear those words. We think life ought to be easy, smooth, comfortable. And, above all, *nice*.

But that's not life . . . that's *Fantasy Island*. That's *Alice in Wonderland* stuff. It's why Disney World is such a unique experience—it is a *departure* from real life, not real life itself.

I know that's not what college admissions officers tell you. It's not their job to say, "Look, these next few years you're gonna live pretty well, but after you graduate, you won't know what hit you."

It's not what car salesmen tell you. It's not their job to tell you, "Friend, the moment you drive this new car off this lot, it will instantly depreciate by about 20 percent."

It's not what you'll hear from a server in a restaurant. It's not that person's job to warn you, "Listen, this shrimp pasta you're ordering has more calories than three sticks of butter, more than 900 milligrams of sodium, and 78 grams of saturated fat. It looks pretty and healthy, I know, but it is roughly the same as eating four Big Macs in one sitting."

But *Qoheleth* is none of those things. He is going to tell you the way things really are, even if they're unpleasant to read or hear. And he gives you the naked truth from the perspective of many years, and many hard-learned lessons.

This book of Ecclesiastes would not have been written by a young man. Shoot, when you're young, you think the world is your oyster. But as the years go by, you realize more and more that you can pursue happiness all you want, but sadness will find you one way or another. You can eat right and exercise, but you won't hold off disease or old age forever. You can treat people the way you want to be treated, but some folks aren't going to like you no matter what you do. As psychologist Sheldon Kopp wrote, "Life can be counted on to provide all the pain that any of us might need."[78]

So is that it? Is that all there is? Do we just resign ourselves to "Life stinks . . . and then you die"?

No.

That is *not* the message of Ecclesiastes. It may sound like that from time to time as you're reading, because it is an exploration, a philosophical reverie. But *Qoheleth*'s message can actually encourage us and take us to a new place. And the third chapter of Ecclesiastes supplies us with four intensely practical things to cultivate that will equip us to live life well even in the midst of a sick world—if we take its wisdom to heart and apply it to our lives.

Cultivate the Faith to Accept God's Timing

It is crucial to recognize that the first eight verses of Ecclesiastes 3 aren't *telling us what to do*. If that were the case, some of these verses would contradict clear commands of Scripture. But that is not the case. *Qoheleth* isn't *telling us what to do*; he is simply *telling it like it is*.

You see, ultimately, *we* don't decide the time to be born or die, the time to plant or uproot, and so on. Those things come to us at times of *God's* choosing. As Solomon's father, King David, once sang to God, "My times are in your hands."[79]

And while we all want to pray, "God, please let my life be one long string of times to be born, and times to plant; times to heal, and times to build, and laugh, and dance, and so on," we really know better. Or we ought to.

As Job said to his wife after his world had fallen apart, "Shall we accept good from God, and not trouble?"[80] To which most of us would answer, "Yes, please."

We want God to send us only:

Sunday, Monday, Happy Days,
Tuesday, Wednesday, Happy Days,
Thursday, Friday, Happy Days,
Saturday, what a day, groovin' all week with you.[81]

But God never signed off on that deal. He says:

I beg your pardon,
I never promised you a rose garden.
Along with the sunshine,
There's gonna be a little rain sometime.[82]

Maybe you never before heard the voice of God in tones like those of Lynn Anderson or Martina McBride, but that is the gist of the message in Ecclesiastes 3:1:

There is a time for everything,
     and a season for every activity under the heavens.[83]

"True wisdom," writes philosopher Jacques Ellul, "means allowing reality to instruct us."[84] And the reality, says *Qoheleth*, is that even for the richest, wisest, most educated and comfortably situated person of his age, life holds seasons of good and bad, up and down, blessing and tragedy. We should not expect otherwise. "The truth is," said poet and novelist Anatole France, "that life is delicious, horrible, charming, sweet, bitter and that is everything."[85]

In fact, notice that *Qoheleth* lists twenty-eight possible activities, in fourteen pairs:

> being born/dying
> planting/uprooting
> killing/healing
> destroying/constructing
> weeping/laughing
> mourning/dancing
> scattering/gathering
> embracing/refraining
> searching/giving up
> keeping/discarding
> tearing/mending
> being silent/speaking
> loving/hating
> making war/making peace.

Ellul writes:

> It is tempting to think of twenty-eight as seven times four: a seamless totality with no possible additions, involving everything a human being can do. This may well hold some truth. It is difficult to come up with an action or feeling one could add to *Qoheleth*'s list. Our entire life, including all our activities, boils down to precisely those twenty-eight starting points.[86]

Most of us see roughly half of *Qoheleth*'s list as normal, and the other half as aberrations. But they are all normal. Birth, death, weeping, laughing, acquiring, and losing are all part of the normal course of things. We cannot completely avoid any of them; we shouldn't expect to. But we can cultivate the faith to accept God's timing.

Are you in a season of gathering? Praise God . . . and cultivate the faith to accept this season as well as the next, which may be a time of scattering.

Are you enduring a period of loss? Lean on God . . . and cultivate the faith to accept this season while awaiting the next, which may be a season of joy.

Are you suffering through discord and division right now? Pray for faith to see God's purpose in it all, even as you look for the dawn of a new era of peace in your relationships.

Rather than carping and complaining when the cycles and seasons of life hit us hard, we should cultivate the faith to believe that God knows what he is doing, his intentions are good, and his timing is wise. In his book *A Twentieth Century Testimony*, Malcolm Muggeridge wrote:

> Contrary to what might be expected, I look back on experiences that at the time seemed especially desolating and painful with particular satisfaction. Indeed, I can say with complete truthfulness that everything I have learned in my seventy-five years in this world, everything that has truly enhanced and enlightened my existence, has been through affliction and not through happiness, whether pursued or attained. In other words, if it ever were to be possible to eliminate affliction from our earthly existence by means of some drug or other medical mumbo jumbo, as Aldous Huxley envisaged in *Brave New World*, the

result would not be to make life delectable, but to make it too banal and trivial to be endurable.[87]

It is natural to wish only for seasons of laughter and prosperity. It is also shortsighted. It is far better, wiser, and more conducive to living well in this sick world to cultivate the faith to accept God's timing.

Cultivate the Wisdom to Accomplish God's Priorities

After thoroughly cataloguing the unpredictable ups and downs of human experience, *Qoheleth* goes on in Ecclesiastes 3 to say this:

> What do workers gain from their toil? I have seen the burden God has laid on the human race. He has made everything beautiful in its time. He has also set eternity in the human heart; yet no one can fathom what God has done from beginning to end. I know that there is nothing better for people than to be happy and do good while they live. That each of them may eat and drink, and find satisfaction in all their toil—this is the gift of God. I know that everything God does will endure forever; nothing can be added to it and nothing taken from it. God does it so that people will revere him.
>
> > Whatever is has already been,
> > and what will be has been before;
> > and God will call the past to account.[88]

The picture is this: the great King Solomon, the seeker after truth, is at the end of his life, looking back on all he's worked for, all he has built. And as he does, he frowns. Shakes his head. Maybe even groans. Maybe his thoughts turn once more to his son and heir, about whom he wrote in chapter 2:

> I hated all the things I had toiled for under the sun, because
> I must leave them to the one who comes after me. And who
> knows whether that person will be wise or foolish?[89]

He is probably being subtle. Maybe even sarcastic. If you were to read 2 Chronicles 10 in your Bible, you would quickly find out that Solomon's son and heir, Rehoboam, was a ninny. He wasn't wise. He wasted no time in making a series of bonehead decisions with far-reaching consequences.

I bet Solomon saw that coming. That's the backdrop of these words in chapter 3. The king looks at all he's worked for and thinks two things: only what God does really lasts, and I should have enjoyed it more while I had it. I should have found satisfaction in working hard, in doing good, in being happy, living in the moment instead of always stressing about the future.

So wise.

You see, if your priority is amassing a fortune, you're going to end up like Solomon someday, saying, "What was I thinking?" If your priority is cigarettes, whiskey, and wild, wild women, you're going to end up asking, "What was I thinking?" If your priority is winning awards, expanding your business, or getting to the next level of the *Ring of Honor* video game, you're going to end up asking, "What was I thinking?"

Nothing like that will satisfy. We are wired for so much more than we realize. We are intended for eternal purposes. So we should cultivate the wisdom to accomplish God's priorities, to be happy and do good while we live, to enjoy what we've got . . . while we've got it. To live our lives and do our work in the light of eternity.

Qoheleth says, "Everything God does will endure forever."[90] The corollary to that is that the things we do—won't. The things I worked so hard to pay off won't last forever. My job won't last forever. My home won't last forever. My paycheck *definitely* won't last forever.

But my wife will. My children will. My grandchildren will. My friends and neighbors and co-workers will. Eternity knocks on my door every day in the form of the people God places in my path. If Scripture teaches me anything, it tells me that people are important to God. So when I make my wife a priority (or my kids, grandkids, friends, etc.), I can more heartily and happily enjoy all God's gifts—eating and drinking and working—because I am pursuing God's priorities.

Cultivate the Patience to Await God's Judgment

Qoheleth continues, in verses 16–17, to say this:

> And I saw something else under the sun:
>
> > In the place of judgment—wickedness was there,
> >   in the place of justice—wickedness was there.
>
> I said to myself,
>
> > "God will bring to judgment
> >   both the righteous and the wicked,
> > for there will be a time for every activity,
> >   a time for every deed."[91]

This guy doesn't mince words. He says, basically, "Know what else I've figured out? Everybody's crooked. Everybody's on the take. Everybody's running some kinda scam."

There's probably not a man or woman among us who hasn't complained:

"How did *she* get elected prom queen?"

"How could they promote *him*, of all people?"

"How could anyone vote for *that* joker?"

"How come *she's* not behind bars?"

"I'd sure like to see *him* get what's coming to him."

Not me, of course. Not you. But we understand why *other* people think such things. It is no different today than it was in Solomon's day, which is why we must cultivate the faith to await God's judgment.

God's Word promises that a day is coming when

> God "will give to each person according to what he has done." To those who by persistence in doing good seek glory, honor and immortality, he will give eternal life. But for those who are self-seeking and who reject the truth and follow evil, there will be wrath and anger.[92]

Sure, life stinks when it seems like wicked people are just whizzing by you on the ladder of success. Life stinks when your lazy neighbor wins the lottery . . . when your roommate, who never studies, gets a scholarship . . . when your brother gets a car for his sixteenth birthday, and you didn't even get a *card* because you were working with Mother Teresa among the poor of Calcutta.

These are all the reasons we need to cultivate the patience to await God's judgment. Don't expect God to sort things out right here, right now. Jesus said:

> The kingdom of heaven is like a man who sowed good seed in his field. But while everyone was sleeping, his enemy came and sowed weeds among the wheat, and went away. When the wheat sprouted and formed heads, then the weeds also appeared.
>
> The owner's servants came to him and said, "Sir, didn't you sow good seed in your field? Where then did the weeds come from?"
>
> "An enemy did this," he replied.
>
> The servants asked him, "Do you want us to go and pull them up?"

"No," he answered, "because while you are pulling the weeds, you may root up the wheat with them. Let both grow together until the harvest. At that time I will tell the harvesters: First collect the weeds and tie them in bundles to be burned; then gather the wheat and bring it into my barn."[93]

In other words, Jesus said, "be *glad* it's not yet judgment time, because you've still got that whole weed-looking thing going on yourself!" In an echo of the poem that opened Ecclesiastes 3, *Qoheleth* promises "there will be a time for every activity, a time for every deed."[94] But that time is not yet. So pray, wait, and cultivate the patience to await God's judgment.

Cultivate the Hope to Anticipate God's Reward

All the above leaves us just a few more verses and one more wise action to take for those of us who are getting all dizzy in the "circle of life." Ecclesiastes 3:18–22 says:

I also said to myself, "As for humans, God tests them so that they may see that they are like the animals. Surely the fate of human beings is like that of the animals; the same fate awaits them both: As one dies, so dies the other. All have the same breath; humans have no advantage over animals. Everything is meaningless. All go to the same place; all come from dust, and to dust all return. Who knows if the human spirit rises upward and if the spirit of the animal goes down into the earth?"

So I saw that there is nothing better for a person than to enjoy their work, because that is their lot. For who can bring them to see what will happen after them?[95]

Wow. That sorta sounds like *Qoheleth* didn't believe in heaven, right? Like he didn't believe in the immortality of the human soul.

As a matter of fact, at the time Ecclesiastes was written, belief in life after death was not widespread among Jews. But King Solomon's father, David, apparently had that faith, because he wrote,

> Surely goodness and love will follow me all the days of my life, and I will dwell in the house of the LORD forever.[96]

And *Qoheleth* himself has already written, earlier in chapter 3,

> God has . . . planted eternity in the human heart, but even so, people cannot see the whole scope of God's work from beginning to end.[97]

So it is in that context—that people cannot see the whole scope of God's work, that *Qoheleth* is evaluating everything "under the sun"— that this seeker after truth says,

> Who knows if the human spirit rises upward and if the spirit of the animal goes down into the earth?[98]

From an earthbound perspective, we have no way to conclusively determine that we're any different from the animals. Sure, we live in a post–*Touched by an Angel* day and age, a post–*Heaven Is for Real* era. But we still "see through a glass, darkly,"[99] as the Bible says. None of us knows empirically; the only way to get there, really, is by faith. As the Bible says,

> Now faith is being sure of what we hope for and certain of what we do not see.[100]

So living well in a sick world requires us to cultivate the hope to anticipate God's reward. If this life "under the sun" is all there is, then it's all meaningless. If nothing else awaits us, then yeah, it stinks. If my life amounts to nothing more than seventy or eighty years of struggle here and now, then I'm no different than the animals. Better to be a giant tortoise . . . at least they get more than a hundred years.

But I don't believe this life is all there is, and I bet you don't either. I think we all have the sense Thornton Wilder expressed in *Our Town*, when he wrote:

> Now there are some things we all know, but we don't take 'm out and look at 'm very often. We all know that *something* is eternal. And it ain't houses and it ain't names, and it ain't earth, and it ain't even the stars . . . everybody knows in their bones that something is eternal, and that something has to do with human beings. All the greatest people ever lived have been telling us that for five thousand years and yet you'd be surprised how people are always losing hold of it. There's something way down deep that's eternal about every human being.[101]

Everybody knows it in their bones. Even *Qoheleth*, who lived in a time before *It's a Wonderful Life*, had a sense of it. And living day by day in that hope is one of the keys to a life well lived, even in an unwell world.

Do you have that hope? You can, by praying a simple prayer of faith. You can say:

> God, I confess that I am a sinner, just like everyone else on
>   earth.
> But I am willing and ready to turn from my sins
> and accept Jesus' death on the cross as payment for my sin.
> I ask for your forgiveness, based on what Jesus has done,
> and ask you to come into my heart
> and make me a new person
> and take control of my life from this day forward.

>With your Holy Spirit living in me and helping me,
>I commit my life to following Christ,
>in whose name I pray, amen.

It is possible to live, day by day, not seeing "the whole scope of God's work from beginning to end,"[102] not seeing what will happen after your lifetime,[103] but still resting in the hope that "goodness and love will follow me all the days of my life, and I will dwell in the house of the LORD forever."[104] That is a key perspective to living well in a sick world, without getting woozy and wobbly in the "circle of life."

———— ∼ ————

*G*racious Lord, give me the faith, I pray: faith to accept your timing. Grant me the faith to praise and thank you and trust you in all the seasons of this life. Grant me the faith not to carp and complain when the normal cycles of life hit me hard and sorely try me. Grant me the faith to believe that you know what you are doing, that your intentions are good, and that your timing is wise.

Please help me also to cultivate the wisdom to accomplish your priorities, not my own. As Jesus prayed, "Not my will, but yours."[105] Teach me to be happy and do good while I live, to enjoy what I've got while I've got it, and to live my life and do my work in the light of eternity, remembering that everything you do will endure forever.[106]

Also, Lord, give me the patience to await your judgment. Let me always be among those who persist in doing good,[107] while praying for those "who are self-seeking and who reject the truth and follow evil"[108] and leaving them in your hands, knowing that you will bring to judgment both the righteous and the wicked.[109]

And finally, please help me to cultivate the hope to anticipate your reward, living in the awareness that this world and this life are not all there is, and resting in the confident assurance that "goodness and love will follow me all the days of my life, and I will dwell in the house of the LORD forever."[110] In Jesus' name, amen.

THE SMARTER I GET, THE LESS I KNOW

When my wife, the lovely Robin, and I welcomed our children into the world, I had a grand plan to pass on all my wisdom to those two kids. I would teach them everything I knew, and someday they would look up at me and say, "Oh, wise father, speak, for we are listening."

That never happened.

Instead, I regularly call my kids (who are now both adults, with children of their own) for advice with a sermon or computer or a book manuscript.

And it's not just me.

My friend Shery would tell you that when she was younger, she thought chocolate was a nice occasional treat. Now that she's a little older and wiser, she knows that chocolate is one of the basic food groups.

My friend Scott says when he was younger, he knew people's names and faces. Nowadays, he knows their faces, but their names? Not so much.

My friend Vi says when she was younger, she knew what love was; now she has learned enough to know that true love is much, much more than she can comprehend. Kevin says when he was a kid, he thought his schoolteachers were old; now, he realizes they weren't old at all. Patty expected when she was younger that with age would come all the answers she craved—especially in spiritual things—but now she says she has more questions than ever.

I can identify. To very loosely paraphrase the prophet Joni Mitchell, "I've looked at life from all sides now, and all I've learned is that I really don't know jack about life." In fact, the smarter I get, the less I know.

King Solomon's alter ego, *Qoheleth,* said much the same thing in his tone poem on life, wisdom, success, and satisfaction in the book of Ecclesiastes. In words attributed to Solomon, who has been revered for three thousand years as the paragon of wisdom, the smartest man who ever lived, *Qoheleth* outlines for us three pursuits that typically possess men and women in their early years, pursuits that seem to offer meaning, value, fulfillment, and hope. But then, after mentioning each one, he artfully describes a better approach each of us can take, one that is less frustrating, more worthwhile, and far more productive than the path more commonly taken.

Don't Let Injustice Overwhelm You

One of the most common passions of youth is a passion for justice.

How old do you think you were when you first learned to say, "That's not fair!" or "Take that back!" or "So's your old man!"

Okay, so that last one may be more than a little outdated, but you get the idea. There is a reason most revolutions and protest movements start among the young. They have a keen sense of fair play, and they will fight for justice with exuberance.

But the author of Ecclesiastes, the "seeker" who wrote this book, says:

Again I looked and saw all the oppression that was taking place under the sun:

> I saw the tears of the oppressed—
>> and they have no comforter;
> power was on the side of their oppressors—
>> and they have no comforter.
> And I declared that the dead,
>> who had already died,
> are happier than the living,
>> who are still alive.
> But better than both
>> is the one who has never been born,
> who has not seen the evil
>> that is done under the sun.

And I saw that all labor and all achievement spring from one person's envy of another. This too is meaningless, a chasing after the wind.

> Fools folds their hands
>> and ruin themselves.
> Better one handful with tranquility
>> than two handfuls with toil
>> and chasing after the wind.

Again I saw something meaningless under the sun:

> There was a man all alone;
>> he had neither son nor brother.

> There was no end to his toil,
>   yet his eyes were not content with his wealth.
> "For whom am I toiling," he asked,
>   "and why am I depriving myself of enjoyment?"
> This too is meaningless—
>   a miserable business![111]

Anyone who lived through the 1960s could easily picture the author of Ecclesiastes as a hippie. He sounds much like that great theologian, Bob Dylan, who sang:

> Half-wracked prejudice leaped forth
> "Rip down all hate," I screamed.
> Lies that life is black and white
> Spoke from my skull . . . somehow.
> Ah, but I was so much older then,
> I'm younger than that now.[112]

If you have lived to adulthood without feeling outrage at the injustice that pervades this sick world in which we live, something is wrong. Injustice is everywhere. It can be overwhelming. But *Qoheleth* says . . .

Don't Let Injustice Overwhelm You . . . Cultivate Community

Injustice thrives where alienation, miscommunication, and mistrust have taken root. So the antidote to injustice is community. Togetherness. Communication. Understanding. As *Qoheleth* says in verses 9–12 of Ecclesiastes 4:

> Two are better than one,
>   because they have a good return for their labor:
> If either of them falls down,
>   one can help the other up.

> But pity anyone who falls
> > and has no one to help them up!
> Also, if two lie down together, they will keep warm.
> > But how can one keep warm alone?
> Though one may be overpowered,
> > two can defend themselves.
> A cord of three strands is not quickly broken.[113]

The wisdom of these words is amazing. In a world where injustice is so rampant, so incessant, so overwhelming, we can get so wrapped up in cursing the darkness that we never light any candles. So *Qoheleth* says, don't let injustice overwhelm you; cultivate community instead.

Notice *Qoheleth*'s progression of thought in those verses. He starts with one ("if one falls down"), proceeds to two ("if two lie down together"), and ends up at three ("a cord of three strands"). This is typical of Hebrew poetry, and it is an artful depiction of the value of community. Two are better than one. A loving community is better than a lone cowboy.

Japanese filmmaker Akira Kurosawa's cinematic masterpiece, *Ran*, contains a scene in which the aging Hidetora prepares to divide his feudal kingdom among his three sons, an action fraught with peril and likely to produce jealousy and competition among his heirs. So he hands each of his sons a single arrow and tells them to break it, which they do easily. Then he hands them a bundle of three arrows to emphasize that the three brothers will be far stronger if they are united. "Though one may be overpowered, two can defend themselves. A cord of three strands is not quickly broken."[114] And we become stronger and better—and our world does, too—when we learn to live in community with others.

This is why involvement in and commitment to the local church is so critical to living well in a sick world. In his book, *Courageous Leadership,* Pastor Bill Hybels writes:

I had just finished presenting my weekend message . . . and I was standing [up front]. A young married couple approached me, placed a blanketed bundle in my arms, and asked me to pray for their baby.

As I asked what the baby's name was, the mother pulled back the blanket that had covered the infant's face. I felt my knees begin to buckle. I thought I was going to faint. . . . In my arms was the most horribly deformed baby I had ever seen. . . .

All I could say was, "Oh my . . . oh my . . . oh my."

"Her name is Emily," said the mother.

"We've been told she has about six weeks to live," added the father. "We would like you to pray that before she dies she will know and feel our love."

Barely able to mouth the words, I whispered, "Let's pray." Together we prayed for Emily. Oh, did we pray. As I handed her back to her parents I asked, "Is there anything we can do for you, any way that we as a church can serve you during this time?"

The father responded . . . "Bill, we're okay. Really we are. We've been in a loving small group for years. Our group members knew that this pregnancy had complications. They were at our house the night we learned the news, and they were at the hospital when Emily was delivered. They helped us absorb the reality of the whole thing. They even cleaned our house and fixed our meals when we brought her home. They pray for us constantly and call us several times a day. They are even helping us plan Emily's funeral."

Just then the three other couples stepped forward and surrounded Emily and her parents. . . .

It was a picture I will carry to my grave.[115]

You can let injustice overwhelm you, but it is far better to pursue community. Not only for you, but for others as well. Because, guess what? When you cultivate community for yourself, you bestow it on others at the same time.

So don't let injustice overwhelm you. Cultivate community instead.

Don't Let Popularity Deceive You

Another common, pervasive pursuit of youth is the pursuit of popularity. And some of us never quite get over it, no matter how successful or admired we become. For many of us, a craving for acceptance and approval translates into adult dysfunctions: we become people pleasers in our homes, jobs, and churches; we find it difficult (or impossible) to say "no"; we become anxious, depressed, or irritable based on social slights from others (real or perceived) or our own personal failures (real or perceived). We may not long for the spotlight, but we wouldn't mind it if someone would notice us and want to be around us.

But the pursuit of popularity is as unsatisfying in adulthood as it is in childhood or youth. *Qoheleth* says:

> Better a poor but wise youth than an old but foolish king
> who no longer knows how to heed a warning. The youth
> may have come from prison to the kingship, or he may
> have been born in poverty within his kingdom. I saw
> that all who lived and walked under the sun followed the
> youth, the king's successor. There was no end to all the
> people who were before them. But those who came later
> were not pleased with the successor. This too is meaning-
> less, a chasing after the wind.[116]

Those four short verses manage to hit all three phrases that occur repeatedly in this unusual book:

> "under the sun,"
> "meaningless,"
> and "chasing after the wind."

That's a trifecta. A hat trick. A triple crown of disillusionment.

If you pursue popularity, whether you're a young buck or an old coot, a pastor or performer (or both!), you will be disappointed, because it is ultimately and utterly unsatisfying. It is a whirlwind of futility. It is like chasing your tail. Instead, this wise seeker after truth urges us . . .

Don't Let Popularity Deceive You . . . Cultivate Faithfulness

An abrupt shift seems to take place with the end of Ecclesiastes 4. In chapter 4, *Qoheleth* has been talking about kings and princes, predecessors and successors, rejection and popularity. Then, as chapter 5 begins, he seems to change the subject completely; he talks about watching your step and watching your mouth when you go to God's house and treating God with respect and reverence.

But though it might seem so at first glance, it is not an abrupt change of subject; it is the flip side of the same coin, so to speak. The first seven verses of Ecclesiastes' fifth chapter actually present an alternative perspective to the pursuit of popularity:

> Guard your steps when you go to the house of God. Go
> near to listen rather than to offer the sacrifice of fools, who
> do not know that they do wrong.
>
> Do not be quick with your mouth,
> do not be hasty in your heart

> to utter anything before God.
> God is in heaven
>   and you are on earth,
>   so let your words be few.
> As a dream comes when there are many cares,
>   and many words mark the speech of a fool.
>
> When you make a vow to God, do not delay to fulfill
> it. He has no pleasure in fools; fulfill your vow. It is better
> not to make a vow than to make one and not fulfill it. Do
> not let your mouth lead you into sin. And do not protest
> to the temple messenger, "My vow was a mistake." Why
> should God be angry at what you say and destroy the
> work of your hands? Much dreaming and many words are
> meaningless. Therefore fear God.[117]

If you want a life that God rewards, stop trying to please people.
If you want to pursue something that will pay dividends sooner or
later, then quiet down and look to God. Seek to please him instead of
other people. Keep your eyes on him. Worship him. Fulfill your vows
to him. Cultivate a lifestyle of worship, reverence, faithfulness, and
sincere, humble submission to God, and you will be much better off.

Don't let popularity deceive you. Cultivate faithfulness instead.

Don't Let the Pursuit of Wealth Consume You

I don't think any of us set out in our twenties to make a hundred
dollars. I sincerely doubt that you graduated from high school or
college and thought, "I'm going to work as hard as I can to get a job
earning minimum wage!" Am I right? Of course I'm right. We all
start out life with at least a little more hope than that. But too often
our hopes and dreams for income get to be like smuggling a Great

Dane puppy into a dorm room—sooner or later it grows too big and takes over everything.

That's why this "seeker after truth," writing in Ecclesiastes, says:

If you see the poor oppressed in a district, and justice and rights denied, do not be surprised at such things; for one official is eyed by a higher one, and over them both are others higher still. The increase from the land is taken by all; the king himself profits from the fields.

Whoever loves money never has enough;
> whoever loves wealth is never satisfied with their
> > income.
> This too is meaningless.

As goods increase,
> so do those who consume them.
And what benefit are they to the owners
> except to feast their eyes on them?

The sleep of a laborer is sweet,
> whether they eat little or much,
but as for the rich, their abundance
> permits them no sleep.

I have seen a grievous evil under the sun:

wealth hoarded to the harm of its owners,
> or wealth lost through some misfortune,
so that when they have children
> there is nothing left for them to inherit.
Everyone comes naked from their mother's womb,
> and as everyone comes, so they depart.
They take nothing from their toil
> that they can carry in their hands.

This too is a grievous evil:

As everyone comes, so they depart,
    and what do they gain,
        since they toil for the wind?
All their days they eat in darkness,
        with great frustration, affliction and anger.[118]

Much as he did in chapter 2, *Qoheleth* makes quite a case against the pursuit of wealth, giving five reasons it is ultimately and utterly unsatisfying.

1. It is eaten up by taxes and fees. "The increase from the land is taken by all; the king himself profits from the fields."[119] Little has changed since Solomon's day—though none of us possess quite his perspective, looking down on a pyramidal tax structure; most of us are at the bottom, looking up! The average American taxpayer works more than three months of the year to pay his or her local, state, federal, payroll, property, and sales taxes. And the harder we work, of course, the more we must pay. The more we add to our income, the larger the percentage we must pay to others.

2. We never get enough. "Whoever loves money never has enough," he says. When I first married my wife, the lovely Robin, I knew that she had a mental list of things she wanted to own someday. For a nineteen-year-old couple (yes, we were married at nineteen, what of it?), it was an ambitious list that included a sewing machine, a bentwood rocking chair, a piano, and six or seven other items. Imagine my excitement when, on her thirtieth birthday, I gave her the last item on the list—a brand new piano! It was so gratifying . . . until I learned that she had a *new* mental list for me to start on right away. Mind you, we weren't terribly materialistic people. And to be fair, she had never promised me (and I had never asked her) that when we acquired everything on that first list, we would call it quits. It's just that our standard of living had increased in those ten-plus years. Few—if any of us—ever reach a point where we can sit back and fold our hands and say, "Finally, we have enough money, enough possessions." No matter how high our salary, we are happy to accept a raise. "Enough" is as difficult to reach as the "bright elusive butterfly of love."[120]

3. It disappears quickly. "As goods increase," *Qoheleth says,* "so do those who consume them."[121] I grew up in a middle class family as the youngest of three boys. My parents often struggled to make ends meet. My older brothers and I remember often laughing and shaking our heads at our mother, who would sometimes exclaim, "I don't know why I bother to buy cookies, because you boys just *eat them.*" Putting aside the injustice of the remark (because our father was as guilty as we were), it was funny at the time because, well, what else is one supposed to do with groceries, right? But now that my brothers and I are all parents (grandparents, in fact), we understand completely. It is dizzying how fast groceries disappear when teenagers (especially) are in the house and disconcerting how quickly money disappears. In fact, in today's "cashless" economy, it often disappears long before payday comes.

4. It becomes a burden. "As for the rich, their abundance permits them no sleep," *Qoheleth* says. I have a friend (seriously, I do). He had already been quite successful in his work life, but in his late forties, he hit the jackpot. With new and unprecedented success came extensive wealth—more than he had ever anticipated. More, in fact, than he was able to spend, at least for a while. But it came with a price. For example, he can't drive a car anymore. If he were involved in a fender bender, the other driver might see even the tiniest accident as an opportunity to cash in. His liability is too great; there are just too many ways for him to be sued. So someone must drive him wherever he goes. His wealth comes with a price tag. It can be a blessing, but it can also be a burden.

5. You can't take it with you. *Qoheleth* made this point back in chapter 2, when he was writing about the futility of losing yourself in work. But he returns to it again as he writes, "Everyone comes naked from their mother's womb, and as everyone comes, so they depart. They take nothing from their toil that they can carry in their hands."[122] A few years ago, I had the opportunity to visit Egypt, before a wave of unrest and uprisings virtually shut down tourism to that amazing country. In addition to (of course) visiting the pyramids and the Sphinx, I toured the Egyptian Museum in Cairo and viewed the breathtakingly beautiful treasures of King Tutankhamun and Ramses and other pharaohs. Much of the museum's priceless collection came from the ancient tombs of Egyptian royalty. The pharaohs stocked their tombs with overflowing riches because the plan was to take those possessions into the afterlife. But of course, when the tombs were discovered and opened millennia later, the treasures were still there. They'd been left behind. And mine will be, too. And so will yours.

For those reasons—and more—the pursuit of wealth will end only in frustration, affliction, and anger. Which is why *Qoheleth* suggests an alternative.

Don't Let the Pursuit of Wealth Consume You . . . Cultivate Contentment

Far better than the frustration, affliction, and anger of the person who is consumed by the pursuit of wealth is the contentment of the man or woman who gratefully accepts and enjoys what God gives:

> This is what I have observed to be good: that it is appropriate for a person to eat, to drink, and to find satisfaction

in their toilsome labor under the sun during the few days
of life God has given them—for this is their lot. Moreover,
when God gives someone wealth and possessions, and the
ability to enjoy them, to accept their lot and be happy in
their toil—this is a gift of God. They seldom reflect on the
days of their life, because God keeps them occupied with
gladness of heart.[123]

A millennium after these words were written, Paul, the great church
planter of the first Christian century, wrote,

Godliness with contentment is great gain.[124]

Contentment doesn't mean you sit on your hands (or other body
part) and eat bon bons all day. It doesn't mean you stop trying to
improve. It doesn't mean you put things on cruise control. However,
it *does* mean pursuing a lifestyle that shows money is your servant,
not your master. As Jesus said,

No one can serve two masters. Either you will hate the
one and love the other, or you will be devoted to the one
and despise the other. You cannot serve both God and
money.[125]

If money is your master, God is not. If God is your master, then money
must be your servant. You must control it, not be controlled by it.

How do you do that, in practical terms? How do you cultivate
contentment when everyone around you seems to be focused on
the pursuit of wealth? Here are three ideas, very practical things I
recommend.

1. Start and end every day by thanking God. Thank him for
everything you have, material things and non-material things. Thank
him for *the things you don't own*—things you don't have to dust, store,

insure, etc. Thank him that money *doesn't own you*. Do it in writing, even, in a journal or on your computer. Paul said,

> In every thing give thanks: for this is the will of God in
> Christ Jesus concerning you.[126]

Don't miss that. It is God's will for you to give thanks. And giving thanks will bring more and more of his will to pass in your life. It will breed contentment (it's hard to be greedy for more when you're truly grateful for what God has given you). It will improve your moods (it's hard to get depressed while reviewing all that God has done for you). And it will draw you closer to God, as a grateful heart is always more open to his presence. I have made it a practice for years to journal five or more "thank you prayers" at the end of each day, an exercise that has helped me immensely in falling asleep, battling depression, and more. If you you need help getting started in this area, I recommend Ann Voskamp's excellent book, *One Thousand Gifts*.

2. Focus more time and effort on things that endure instead of things that decay. Jesus said,

> Put away riches in heaven that will not be used up. There,
> no thief can come near it. There, no moth can destroy it.[127]

Obviously, "riches in heaven" includes your salvation, your relationship with God. But your soul isn't the only thing you can take into eternity with you! You have other heavenly riches, too: children, family members, friends, co-workers, classmates, students. Your relationships are riches that don't decay. What a shame it would be to neglect those enduring riches for the sake of mere money. So focus your time and effort on knowing, loving, and blessing loved ones and friends and other people, rather than making more money.

3. Don't focus on "getting" contentment but on giving. Contentment is a lot like one of those "magic eye" pictures that were popular some years ago. If you focus on a "magic eye" picture, you'll never see the 3-D image embedded somewhere inside. You have to focus on something *beyond* the obvious, something *behind* the surface; only then will you see the fuller picture. When it comes to contentment, if you focus on being content, you won't "get it." But if you focus on something beyond contentment—giving to and blessing others—the fuller picture will take shape. You'll find contentment through giving. Give generously. Give anonymously. Give cheerfully. Give creatively. And you will break chains and cultivate contentment in your life like never before.

As sick as this world is, it is possible to live well. It is possible to love the life you lead. It is possible to eat and drink, to find satisfaction in your work, to enjoy whatever wealth and possessions God gives you, and experience gladness of heart. In fact, it is more than possible. It will become a reality for you as you cultivate community, faithfulness, and contentment.

———— ≈ ————

*W*ise and loving God, it is easy in this life "under the sun" to let injustice overwhelm me. But I ask you, please, to show me how to cultivate community instead. Teach me to pursue togetherness, communication, understanding, and unity with others. Strengthen my involvement in and commitment to my local church, and help me to become stronger and better by living in true community with others, realizing as I do that I am simultaneously blessing others with the blessings of community, too.

I also am prone to letting popularity deceive me. I find success, admiration, acceptance, and approval very attractive. I want to please others, so I find it hard to say no. But I agree with your Word that popularity is meaningless. Help me to seek your approval instead of the approval of those around me. Help me to keep my eyes on you, to please you, and cultivate a lifestyle of faithfulness to you.

I also ask you to deliver me from service and subservience to money and wealth. Teach me, instead of grasping and panting after this world's wealth, to gratefully accept and enjoy what you give, to learn contentment, and to cultivate a lifestyle that shows money to be my servant, not my master.

Help me from this day forward to start and end every day by thanking you. Teach me to focus more time and effort on things that endure instead of things that decay. And focus the eyes of my heart, not on "getting" anything—not even contentment—but on giving, generously, anonymously, cheerfully, and creatively. In Jesus' name, amen.

chapter SIX

MONEY CAN'T BUY HAPPINESS, BUT NEITHER CAN POVERTY

As pastors and church leaders, my wife and I have led or participate in numerous foreign and domestic missions efforts over the years. Every experience is unique and rewarding in multiple ways, both expected and unexpected. But one reaction—at least for Americans—seems completely predictable.

Some years ago, we visited several orphanages in central Mexico with a group from our church. We played and worshiped with the children. We painted, repaired, and improved the facility in which they lived. For part of one trip, my responsibility was commensurate with my skill level: I helped to excavate a clogged sewage pipe and prepare it for replacement (let the record show, however, that *I* was not the person who severed the line at a crucial point and filled the open trench with raw sewage). Every orphanage and church we visited, however, was filled with smiling, charming children, men, and women who stole our hearts.

On a trip to southern Peru, in addition to worship services and evangelistic outreaches, my wife and others shampooed and cut hair for the residents of area pueblos, while I assisted dental teams by cleaning the teeth of the very poor—but often smiling—people of the region. I highly recommend both activities to you, not only as a way to serve others but also to deepen your appreciation for your own dentist and stylist and your comparatively healthy hair and teeth.

On that visit to Peru, I accompanied my pastor friend Don as he visited the people of one of the pueblos his church serves. The homes we entered were beyond basic: tin roofs, block walls, no plumbing, and few comforts. We visited one of the newest church members, a single mother of two children, in her one-room rented house. A single bulb provided light for the room. A single bed. A single table and a single chair. And a single hot plate. We talked, prayed—even laughed—together. By the time our visit was over, the children—though shy at first—dazzled me with their smiles and hugs.

Such experiences stay with you a long time. And I've never known it to fail: at some point in a trip like that, one of the middle-class American Christians in the group will put into words what most or all had been thinking. "They're so poor. They have *nothing*. And yet they're so happy!"

Do you see what those words reveal? The hidden assumption they expose?

Deep down, we think it takes money to be happy. In our heart of hearts, we have trouble believing that someone can be happy though poor. Even if the happiest moments in our personal history occurred when we were poorest—as broke college students or struggling newlyweds, for example—we still somehow expect there to be a causal relationship between wealth and happiness.

More Than Money

But *Qoheleth* repeatedly makes it clear that money can't buy happiness. If it could, certainly Solomon should have been the happiest man on earth. Though the Bible doesn't specify the personal fortune Solomon's father, King David, left him when he died, it does report a legacy of twenty-five billion dollars worth of gold to be used in building and furnishing the Temple in Jerusalem.[128] Whatever fortune Solomon possessed when he began his reign, the Bible says his annual income as king was 666 talents in gold,[129] which equates to about 175 million dollars today. In addition to that sum, he received tax and tribute payments in silver, ivory, exotic animals, and more. So if anyone could chart a connection between money and happiness, Solomon could. If anyone was qualified to expound on the advantages of great wealth, Solomon was.

But he does no such thing.

In fact, he does exactly the opposite. Repeatedly in Ecclesiastes, Solomon's alter ego portrays riches as inadequate or irrelevant to the pursuit of a life that is worth living. More than that, he speaks bluntly of money and possessions as detrimental to a meaningful life. And, in the sixth chapter of his treatise, he recommends three pursuits or perspectives that are preferable to the pursuit of money and wealth. These may be summarized in just three short words: delight, deny, and die.

Delight: Steer Your Heart's Desires

Ecclesiastes 6 begins:

> I have seen another evil under the sun, and it weighs
> heavily on mankind: God gives some people wealth, pos-
> sessions and honor, so that they lack nothing their hearts
> desire, but God does not grant them the ability to enjoy

them, and strangers enjoy them instead. This is meaningless, a grievous evil.[130]

Qoheleth speaks generally of "some people" to whom God grants
wealth, possessions, and honor, but who are unable to enjoy them.
But something in his phrasing suggests that he had one or more specific instances in mind. Maybe he was writing about himself; perhaps these verses are biographical. For example, he may have been
writing from a sickbed while thinking of all the pleasures he could
not enjoy.

I think it's more likely, however, that he had in mind someone
else. He may have been thinking of a member of his court, perhaps.
Or a fellow potentate—some king or queen who had been recently
deposed, leaving all the fruits of his or her labors to others. Or it may
have been such a familiar occurrence in his day and age that he could
have listed several names of people who achieved great wealth, possessions, and honor without being able to long or truly enjoy them.

Have you known or seen anyone like that? Someone who seems
to have obtained his heart's desires and yet is unable to enjoy them?
If you haven't noticed them already, you shouldn't have to look very
far. They are all around you.

In early 1985, Arista Records released an album by a wholesome,
gifted twenty-year-old named Whitney Houston. Her self-titled
debut included the #1 hits, "Saving All My Love for You," "How Will
I Know," and "Greatest Love of All." In no time at all, Houston was at
the top of the music world, owning the best-selling debut album by a
solo performer and becoming the first female artist to top *Billboard*'s
artist of the year and album of the year lists at the end of the year.
From that point on, she enjoyed one success after another: hit songs,
countless awards, movie roles, and more—the modern epitome of
Qoheleth's "wealth, possessions, and honor."

But at the very pinnacle of her success, happiness seemed more elusive for her than ever. Her marriage to R&B singer Bobby Brown was tumultuous. Her behavior became erratic. Evidence of drug abuse seemed undeniable. By the time she starred in the 2005 reality show series, "Being Bobby Brown," her coarse, vulgar, disheveled persona seemed irreconcilable with the pop diva who sang, "I Will Always Love You." And when, in 2012, she was found dead in a Beverly Hills hotel bathtub, the world mourned not only the tragedy of her death, but the sadness of her life. "Meaningless," as *Qoheleth* wrote, "a grievous evil."[131]

Qoheleth's lament, however, is not just a complaint. It contains more wisdom than may be obvious at a glance. It is contained in that central phrase, "God gives some people wealth, possessions and honor, so that they lack nothing their hearts desire, but God does not grant them the ability to enjoy them, and strangers enjoy them instead."[132]

1. Steer your heart's desires away from "wealth, possessions, and honor." *Qoheleth* refers to people who have so much wealth, possessions, and honor that they "lack nothing their hearts desire." In other words, their hearts desired wealth. Their hearts desired possessions. Their hearts desired honor. And God gave all those things to them. But he did not grant the ability to enjoy those things but allowed strangers to come along and enjoy them instead. Seems pretty harsh, doesn't it? As if God is a big cosmic tease, giving a person his heart's desire and then snatching it away before he can enjoy it. But that misses the point.

Henry David Thoreau perceived that humans excel at devising "improved means to unimproved ends."[133] *Qoheleth* would have agreed. It doesn't matter how good I get at acquiring wealth, possessions, and honor; they are unimproved ends. In fact, they are inadequate ends. Or, to be precise, they are not ends at all. They are, as clergyman and poet George Herbert styled them, "frailty" and "dust":

> Lord . . . how do I despise
> What upon trust
> Is styled honour, riches, or fair eyes;
> But is—fair dust!
> I surname them gilded clay,
> Dear earth, fine grass or hay.[134]

"The heart is deceitful above all things,"[135] the Bible says; therefore if I "follow my heart," as the popular phrase goes, I may be deceived into thinking that wealth, possessions, and honor are what I truly desire. But I don't have to "follow my heart"; I "have the mind of Christ,"[136] which can tell my heart where to go and steer my heart's desires into improved ends and worthy pursuits.

2. Steer your heart's desires to God and his will. Just one chapter before *Qoheleth* said, "God gives some people wealth, possessions and honor, so that they lack nothing their hearts desire, but God does not grant them the ability to enjoy them, and strangers enjoy them instead,"[137] he wrote, "When God gives someone wealth and possessions, and the ability to enjoy them, to accept their lot and be happy in their toil—this is a gift of God."[138] Those two verses are like the opposite sides of a coin.

It is a gift from God to acquire wealth and possessions *along with* the ability to enjoy them. But some people seek the gifts, not the giver. A. W. Tozer wrote:

> If God gives you a rose without giving Himself, He is
> giving you a thorn. If God gives you a garden without
> giving Himself, He is giving you a garden with a serpent. If

He gives you wine without the knowledge of God Himself, He is giving you that with which you may destroy yourself.

I feel that we must repudiate this great, modern wave of seeking God for His benefits. The sovereign God wants to be loved for Himself and honored for Himself, but that is only part of what He wants. The other part is that He wants us to know that when we have Him, we have everything—we have all the rest. Jesus made that plain when He said, "Seek ye first the kingdom of God and His righteousness, and all these things shall be added unto you. . . ."

Of course, we believe that God can send money to His believing children—but it becomes a pretty cheap thing to get excited about the money and fail to give the glory to Him who is the Giver!

So many are busy "using" God. Use God to get a job. Use God to give us safety. Use God to give us peace of mind. Use God to obtain success in business. Use God to provide heaven at last.

Brethren, we ought to learn—and learn it very soon—that it is much better to have God first and have God Himself even if we have only a thin dime than to have all the riches and all the influence in the world and not have God with it![139]

"To enjoy the gifts without the giver is idolatry," says author Warren W. Wiersbe, "and this can never satisfy the human heart."[140] God has made us for himself, as Augustine said, and our hearts are restless until they rest in him. To quote eighteenth-century priest St. Vincent Pallotti:

Not the goods of the world, but God.
Not riches, but God.

> Not honors, but God.
> Not distinction, but God.
> Not dignities, but God.
> Not advancement, but God.
> God always and in everything.[141]

When God is "always and in everything" the object of our desire, then and only then can we experience the fulfillment of his promise: "Delight yourself in the LORD, and he will give you the desires of your heart."[142] When that happens, a great irony ensues, as we are enabled to truly and fully enjoy whatever God sends our way—need or plenty,[143] simplicity or abundance, obscurity or advancement—as the gift of God.

Deny: Subdue Your Appetites

Qoheleth goes on building his case, making it clear that wealth, possessions, and honor are unsatisfying ends, in Ecclesiastes 6:3–9:

> A man may have a hundred children and live many years;
> yet no matter how long he lives, if he cannot enjoy his
> prosperity and does not receive proper burial, I say that
> a stillborn child is better off than he. It comes without
> meaning, it departs in darkness, and in darkness its
> name is shrouded. Though it never saw the sun or knew
> anything, it has more rest than does that man—even if
> he lives a thousand years twice over but fails to enjoy his
> prosperity. Do not all go to the same place?
>
> > Everyone's toil is for their mouth,
> >   yet their appetite is never satisfied.
> > What advantage have the wise
> >   over fools?
> > What do the poor gain

> by knowing how to conduct themselves before
> others?
> Better what the eye sees
> than the roving of the appetite.
> This too is meaningless,
> a chasing after the wind.[144]

In *Qoheleth's* day, "a hundred children" would have been considered a passport to comfort and security, as children were (for most people) the only available "social security" or "safety net" for old age. But *Qoheleth* dismisses such prosperity—as well as long life—counting it worthless "if he cannot enjoy his prosperity and does not receive proper burial." And, as we have seen above, such prosperity is empty and unsatisfying unless God is "always and in everything" the object of our desire.

He looks around him and he sees that "everyone's toil is for their mouth, yet their appetite is never satisfied." The Apostle Paul made a similar observation centuries later:

> There are many out there taking other paths, choosing
> other goals, and trying to get you to go along with them.
> I've warned you of them many times; sadly, I'm having to
> do it again. All they want is easy street. They hate Christ's
> Cross. But easy street is a dead-end street. Those who
> live there make their bellies their gods; belches are their
> praise; all they can think of is their appetites.[145]

In recent months, my wife and I have adopted a new nutritional and exercise regimen. Along the way, we've had to confront the fact that we are both sugar addicts. For several months, we eliminated sugar (other than those sugars found naturally in non–processed foods) entirely from our diet. Before long, we were experiencing a range and intensity of flavors we hadn't known for a very long time.

Strawberries, blueberries, peppers, mangoes, and corn tasted surprisingly and satisfyingly sweet. Our food cravings virtually disappeared, and our energy levels increased.

One day, however, I ordered a bowl of oatmeal with my usual mug of black coffee at a favorite cafe near our home. That afternoon and evening, I experienced unusual food cravings. I wasn't hungry, and I wasn't even sure what I wanted to eat; I just knew I wanted *something*. It was all I could think of for the rest of the day. Then I remembered the oatmeal, the first packaged food I had had in some time. So on my next visit to the coffee shop I asked to see the oatmeal package and discovered that one small serving contained 25 grams of sugar! That was all it took to ignite my appetite.

I learned that, for me at least, the only solution is to deny my appetite. I can be perfectly content with three small meals and a small snack or two of healthy food all day—if I stay away from sugar. But if I add just a little sugar in my diet, I will eat and eat, all day long, and never be satisfied.

We may not all be sugar addicts, but we are all "self addicts." Jesus told his disciples, "Whoever wants to be my disciple must deny themselves and take up their cross and follow me."[146] Our appetites will never be satisfied; we must learn to subdue them.

Samuel Logan Brengle, the Salvation Army's "prophet of holiness," saw an example of self-denial in the selection process for Gideon's army, as recorded in Judges 7. Gideon's army of thirty-two thousand faced a formidable Midianite foe of nearly four times their number. But God instructed Gideon to allow any who were afraid to return home, after which only ten thousand remained. God didn't stop there, however. He told Gideon to lead his fighting force to the riverbank and observe how they drank. The vast majority put their mouths directly into the water to drink; only three hundred cupped the water in their hands and lifted it to their mouths. The three hundred, God said, would be the ones Gideon would lead into battle—and to victory over the Midianites. Brengle saw an important truth in that winnowing process.

> These three hundred men meant business. They were not only unafraid, but they were not self-indulgent. They knew how to fight, but they knew something even more important—they knew how to deny themselves. They knew how to deny themselves, not only when there was very little water but when a river rolled at their feet. They were, no doubt, quite as thirsty as the others, but they did not propose to throw down their arms and fall down on their faces to drink in the presence of the enemy. They stood up, kept their eyes open, watched the enemy, kept one hand on shield and bow, while with the other they brought water to their thirsty lips. The other fellows were not afraid to fight, but they . . . were self-indulgent and never dreamed of denying themselves for the common good; so God sent them home along with the fellows who were afraid, and with the three hundred He routed the Midianites.
>
> All mighty men of God have learned to deny them- selves . . . and God has set their souls on fire, helped them to win victory against all odds, and bless the whole world.[147]

The way to live well is not the way of self-indulgence; it is the way of self-denial. To indulge ourselves a little will only ignite our appe- tite and eventually corrupt us, much as Smeagol's lust for the ring transformed him into Gollum in *The Lord of the Rings*. Wealth, possessions, and honor are incapable of satisfying our desires; a life well-lived is not defined by an abundance of possessions,[148] but (to paraphrase Thoreau) by the number of things we can afford to let alone.[149]

Die: Surrender Your Life Completely into Stronger Hands

The sixth chapter of Ecclesiastes concludes with these words:

> Whatever exists has already been named,
>   and what humanity is has been known;
> no one can contend
>   with someone who is stronger.
> The more the words,
>   the less the meaning,
>   and how does that profit anyone?
>
> For who knows what is good for a person in life,
> during the few and meaningless days they pass through
> like a shadow? Who can tell them what will happen under
> the sun after they are gone?[150]

Those lines seem like a departure from the first nine verses of the chapter. It looks like he is no longer talking about wealth, possessions, and honor, but these lines flow logically and perfectly from all that goes before. *Qoheleth* has shown the futility of seeking satisfaction in money and material things; delight is not to be found in those things, but in God himself and God alone. He has shown the frailty of life and the pointlessness of living for our appetites. And now, in these verses, he hints that there is someone who is stronger, who knows what we can't know, and who can help us to live well in a sick world.

Jesus said, "Whoever does not take up their cross and follow me is not worthy of me. Whoever finds their life will lose it, and whoever loses their life for my sake will find it."[151] We usually—and rightly—look at those words as a reference to salvation, to the soul who surrenders his or her life and loyalty to Jesus and receives eternal life in exchange. But those words do not only refer to the experience of salvation; they also have a more daily, ongoing application to our lives. Eugene Peterson's paraphrase of that verse in *The Message* makes that application a little clearer:

> If you don't go all the way with me, through thick and thin, you don't deserve me. If your first concern is to look after yourself, you'll never find yourself. But if you forget about yourself and look to me, you'll find both yourself and me.[152]

Much of our dissatisfaction and disillusionment in life stems from the stress and struggle of trying to get our way and make our lives turn out the way we want. Our first concern is to look after ourselves and pursue the things we think will satisfy. But both *Qoheleth* and Jesus tell us that we need to die to ourselves. We need to lose our lives in order to truly live. We must not only steer our hearts' desires to God and God alone and subdue our appetites, we must also surrender our lives completely and utterly into the hands of the only One who knows what man really is, who is strong enough to bend earthly circumstances and situations to his will, who knows what is good for a person in life during the few and meaningless days they pass through like a shadow, and who can not only predict but also prescribe what will happen in the future.

The thirty-second chapter of Genesis contains a fascinating account of an incident in the life of the patriarch Jacob. The context is crucial for understanding the story. Jacob, who years before had repeatedly wronged his twin brother and stolen one blessing after another from him, is returning to his homeland and anticipating a reunion with Esau. In his years away from home, Jacob had prospered in wealth, possessions, and honor.

But now, returning to his homeland with huge flocks of sheep and goats, great herds of camels, cattle, and donkeys, along with two wives, numerous servants, and eleven sons, Jacob is afraid for his life. All his wealth, all he has achieved—even his life and the lives of those he loves—could be taken from him if Esau decides to exact revenge. So Jacob prays:

> O God of my father Abraham, God of my father Isaac, LORD, you who said to me, "Go back to your country and your relatives, and I will make you prosper," I am unworthy of all the kindness and faithfulness you have shown your servant. I had only my staff when I crossed this Jordan, but now I have become two camps. Save me, I pray, from the hand of my brother Esau, for I am afraid he will come and attack me, and also the mothers with their children.[153]

But he is still afraid. He is unsure of the outcome. So, even though he has prayed, he stacks the deck, so to speak, and tries to wrangle a peaceful settlement in his own strength, with his own cleverness. He sends part of his caravan ahead in separate groups to buy Esau's favor before they ever meet. He sends his family and remaining possessions ahead and camps alone overnight. And then, somehow, at some point, he is no longer alone:

> So Jacob was left alone, and a man wrestled with him till daybreak. When the man saw that he could not overpower him, he touched the socket of Jacob's hip so that his hip was wrenched as he wrestled with the man. Then the man said, "Let me go, for it is daybreak."
>
> But Jacob replied, "I will not let you go unless you bless me."
>
> The man asked him, "What is your name?"

"Jacob," he answered.

Then the man said, "Your name will no longer be Jacob, but Israel, because you have struggled with God and with humans and have overcome."

Jacob said, "Please tell me your name."

But he replied, "Why do you ask my name?" Then he blessed him there.

So Jacob called the place Peniel, saying, "It is because I saw God face to face, and yet my life was spared."

The sun rose above him as he passed Peniel, and he was limping because of his hip.[154]

Jacob had all the wealth, possessions, and honor a man could have asked for in that day and age. He even had a relationship with God, and he had prayed to God and asked for his help. So why did the "man" show up in the night? Why did Jacob have to wrestle with him? What was the point of it all?

He had to die.

He had to contend with someone who was stronger.

He had to meet—face to face—the One who knows what is good for people in life during the few and meaningless days they pass through like a shadow.

He was not ready to meet his brother as a rich man; he had to do it as a wounded man, a limping man, a man whose life was no longer his own—a dead man. As it turned out, Esau welcomed his prodigal brother with open arms, but it may have turned out differently if Jacob had not approached him, limping, in humble awareness of his poverty and powerlessness.

And the same is true of me. And you.

We are like Jacob. We stress and strive for years, pursuing wealth, possessions, and honor. Sometimes we even hurt those we love to get where we want to go. But sooner or later we must come to a point like the man E. Stanley Jones describes:

> A man promised a pastor that he would not drink again. After the pledge had been taken the man appeared in late evening and said he must be allowed to drink, or he would die. The pastor told him to go home and die, and went on with his work. The next day the man appeared with a new confidence in his face and said, "I died last night." He had, but a new man was alive.[155]

We must die. We must contend with one who is stronger. We must surrender our lives completely and utterly into the hands of the only One who knows what we really are, who is strong enough to bend earthly circumstances and situations to his will, who knows what is good for us, and who can not only predict but also prescribe what will happen in the future.

If we do not, we will never be satisfied. Only by steering our hearts' desires in the right direction, subduing our appetites, and surrendering ourselves can we learn to live well in a sick world.

———————— ❧ ————————

*O*h, my Lord, teach me well the truth of this chapter, that it doesn't matter how good I get at acquiring wealth, possessions, and honor, for they are gilded clay, earth, grass, and hay. Steer my heart's desires away from them and replace those desires with a passion for you and your will. Give me the grace to know that it is much better to have you—even if I have only a thin dime—than to have all the riches and influence in the world and not have you with it! Turn my heart, Lord, until I want:

Not the goods of the world, but God.
Not riches, but God.
Not honors, but God.
Not distinction, but God.
Not dignities, but God.
Not advancement, but God.
God always and in everything.[156]

Teach me to deny myself and subdue my appetites. Cure me of my addiction to "self." And help me to surrender my life completely into your strong hands, you who alone knows what humans really are, who is strong enough to bend earthly circumstances and situations to your will, who knows what is good for me, and who can not only predict but also prescribe what will happen in the future. I do, Lord. I do surrender, just as I am, I give my life into your hands. In Jesus' name, amen.

TOO SOON OLD,
TOO LATE SMART

When I was in high school—don't laugh, it wasn't that long ago—the world was cooling. Top scientists were warning of a coming "ice age." *Time, Newsweek,* and *The New York Times*—even NASA—said so.

More recently, of course, scientists and journalists have warned us of an impending warming crisis—or, still more recently, "global climate change," which encompasses cooling and warming trends, as well as hurricanes, earthquakes, and other variations in the weather.

Not that long ago, everybody knew that coffee was bad for you, especially if you were a kid. I wasn't allowed to drink as a child because, my 6′ 2″ father explained, it would stunt my growth. Now it turns out that coffee's good for you; drinking two cups a day can protect you against diabetes, Parkinson's disease, gallstones, liver disease, and even some cancers.

Back in the 1950s, advertisements for Camel cigarettes included pictures of smiling medical professionals with the following news:

> Family physicians, surgeons, diagnosticians, nose and
> throat specialists, doctors in every branch of medicine
> . . . a total of 113,597 doctors . . . were asked the ques-
> tion: "What cigarette do you smoke?" And more of them
> named Camel as their smoke than any other cigarette!
> Three independent research groups found this to be a fact.
> You see, doctors too smoke for pleasure. That full Camel
> flavor is just as appealing to a doctor's taste as to yours . . .
> that marvelous Camel mildness means just as much to his
> throat as to yours.[157]

It wasn't just Camels, of course. Chesterfield ads boasted "NOW—
Scientific Evidence on Effects of Smoking" and cited research that
found "no adverse effects on the nose, throat and sinuses of the group
from smoking Chesterfield."[158] Nowadays, of course, we know better.
Smoking is bad for you. Even secondhand smoke is bad for you. Even
seeing smoke on a movie screen is bad for you. In fact, even me *writing the word* is probably bad for you.

Former U.S. Health and Human Services Secretary Tommy
Thompson described how he would get so annoyed at the frequency
with which some scientific report would say, "this food is good for
you," and then about six months later another scientific report would
come out saying, "no, that food is bad for you."

So as Health and Human Services Secretary he decided he was in
a position to do something about it. He impaneled a group of renowned
scientists from all over the world to conduct a definitive study that
would eliminate all the conjecture and contradiction. The group studied all sorts of diets from all sorts of cultures. They found out that the
Japanese eat a lot of rice, drink a lot of sake, and suffer fewer heart
attacks than the British and Americans. They learned that Mexicans
eat a lot of corn and tamales, drink a lot of tequila, and suffer fewer
heart attacks than the British and Americans. They saw that Africans

drink very little red wine and eat a lot of wild meat and suffer fewer heart attacks than the British and Americans. The French and Italians drink large amounts of red wine and eat lots of white bread, and they, too, suffer fewer heart attacks than the British and Americans. The Germans eat lots of sausages, lots of fats, drink lots of beer, and *they also* suffer fewer heart attacks than the British and Americans. So after much study and deliberation, he presented at the Abraham Lincoln Unity Dinner in 2007 that their conclusion was: eat and drink whatever you like; speaking English is apparently what kills you.

We Don't Quite Know Everything

One of the most often-quoted lines of movie dialogue in our home as our children were growing up comes from the animated Rankin-Bass production, *'Twas the Night Before Christmas.* At one point in the story, a young know-it-all mouse named Albert claims that only children believe in Santa Claus, prompting Father Mouse to say, "Don't quite know everything, do you?"

That is *Qoheleth*'s message in the seventh and eighth chapters of Ecclesiastes. Thematically—though not numerically—these chapters are the center of *Qoheleth*'s treatise on life, fulfillment, meaning, and purpose. They may seem at first reading to be disjointed thoughts on unrelated subjects. But it is possible to see a pattern and purpose in them, and that is by recognizing one key word, meditating on three key questions, and concluding with one key thought.

The key word to recognize is "better." Warren W. Wiersbe points out that *Qoheleth* uses the word at least eleven times in this chapter. The three key questions are spaced throughout these three central chapters (6:8, 7:13, and 8:1). And the concluding thought is found in the last two verses of chapter 8. The questions and the conclusion suggest to us a "do" or a "don't" that will serve us well as we navigate this life "under the sun" and try to live well in a sick world.

The first question suggests to us a "don't," something *not* to do, something to avoid.

Don't Rely Solely on Human Wisdom

The first of our three questions for consideration occurred back in chapter 6, which we explored in the last chapter. It said,

> What advantage have the wise over fools?[159]

It is a question *Qoheleth* asks repeatedly, and it is especially salient in light of the words with which *Qoheleth* ended the sixth chapter (though the author did not create the chapter divisions; they were added long afterward):

> For who knows what is good for a person in life, during
> the few and meaningless days they pass through like a
> shadow? Who can tell them what will happen under the
> sun after they are gone?[160]

In other words, "life stinks . . . and then you die." It's right there, in the Bible! It is not only stated; it is repeated. But interestingly, the author of this book, this seeker after truth, doesn't stop there. He goes on, after questioning the value of wisdom, to actually list a few examples of human wisdom, a dozen very wise proverbs, in the first twelve verses of chapter 7:

> A good name is better than fine perfume,
>   and the day of death better than the day of birth.
> It is better to go to a house of mourning
>   than to go to a house of feasting,
> for death is the destiny of everyone;
>   the living should take this to heart.
> Sorrow is better than laughter,
>   because a sad face is good for the heart.

The heart of the wise is in the house of mourning,
    but the heart of fools is in the house of pleasure.
It is better to heed the rebuke of a wise person
    than to listen to the song of fools.
Like the crackling of thorns under the pot,
    so is the laughter of fools.
    This too is meaningless.

Extortion turns a wise person into a fool,
    and a bribe corrupts the heart.

The end of a matter is better than its beginning,
    and patience is better than pride.
Do not be quickly provoked in your spirit,
    for anger resides in the lap of fools.

Do not say, "Why were the old days better than these?"
    For it is not wise to ask such questions.[161]

There's wisdom in those verses, for sure. And such wisdom—even if it's human wisdom, even if it has its limits—is a good thing. In verses 11 and 12, he says:

Wisdom, like an inheritance, is a good thing
    and benefits those who see the sun.
Wisdom is a shelter,
    as money is a shelter,
but the advantage of knowledge is this:
    Wisdom preserves those who have it.[162]

Remember, this book of Ecclesiastes is attributed to the guy who was told by God, "Ask for whatever you want me to give you,"[163] who answered by asking for a discerning heart, for wisdom—and was granted his prayer—and more besides![164]

So these verses show the results of Solomon's request. They cat-alog a small sample of his wisdom. A good name *is* better than per-fume (and longer lasting). It *is* better to go to a house of mourning than a house of feasting, if only to remind ourselves of the precious brevity of life. Frustration *is* better than laughter when we use our frustrations to improve things. It is always better to heed the rebuke of the wise. It is always better to finish well. It is always better to be patient than proud.

It may be that Solomon's alter ego is saying, "See? I made the right choice. I was tempted to ask for wealth, but if I had done that, I would've gotten rich but not wise. I considered asking for honor, but then I would've been given honor but not wisdom. I was tempted to ask for long life, but then I would've lived long—as a fool. But by pleasing God by asking for wisdom, I got wisdom *and* riches *and* honor *and* long life."

So, yes, wisdom is a *good* thing. It is a shelter. It is a refuge. A huge advantage. Of great value. Especially to the person who knows its limitations. A wise man or woman will be wise enough not to rely on human wisdom, but will look beyond it.

Do Trust Explicitly in God's Wisdom

Ecclesiastes 7:13 is the second of the three questions that are key to this passage. And it suggests a "do" to us, something to *try*, some-thing to pursue:

> Consider what God has done:
>   Who can straighten
>   what he has made crooked?[165]

There is a lie of the devil that sprouts every so often in the human heart and whispers, "I am a god, I am in control, I can understand all," like the prideful lie that led to Lucifer's fall:

I will ascend to heaven,
I will raise my throne
    above the stars of God,
I will sit enthroned on the mount of assembly,
    on the utmost heights of the sacred mountain.
I will ascend above the tops of the clouds;
I will make myself like the Most High.[166]

Nearly every time I fly in an airplane, I think, *how amazing is this? A man-made machine,* weighing a bajillion tons, that can lift off the ground and fly. Wow. Or take the invention of the atomic bomb in the 1940s, or the release of the iPhone in mid-2007 and the iPad in 2010. Human wisdom, exploration, invention, and innovation have already taken us amazing places.

And yet, as impressive as human wisdom might be,

Who can straighten
    what [God] has made crooked?[167]

The more we discover, the more knowledge we accumulate, the more wisdom we develop, the more our eyes are opened to the limits of our wisdom, to the vast quantity of things we can't understand, maybe never will understand.

Can you imagine standing under the aurora borealis, watching the brilliant shimmer of light caused by charged particles colliding with atoms high in the atmosphere overhead and not hear God saying, "Don't quite know everything, do you?"

Can you imagine swimming amid the dazzling colors of the Great Barrier Reef, stretching for 1,600 miles, the largest single structure on Earth made by single organisms and not hear God saying, "Don't quite know everything, do you?"

Can you imagine hearing the roar and feeling the spray of Niagara Falls in North America, Angel Falls in South America, or Victoria Falls in Africa . . .

Or gazing upon one of the great Redwoods of northern California . . .

Or peering through a telescope at the spiral galaxy NGC 6872, which stretches 522,000 light-years from one end to the other, more than five times the length of our own Milky Way . . .

And not hear God saying, "Don't quite know everything, do you?"

Albert Einstein, one of the world's greatest minds, amazed the world with his theory of special relativity, which led to his theory of general relativity, which opened the door for the discovery of quantum theory, which is characterized by the *uncertainty principle*, which states that Einstein's theories don't apply to objects traveling at extremely high speeds.

Why? We don't know, but it's sort of like driving a car that goes left when you turn the steering wheel left and right when you turn the steering wheel right—until you go faster than 80 mph, and then turning the wheel left puts you in yesterday, and turning the wheel right gets you to tomorrow!

Confused? So am I. So are we all.

"When times are good," *Qoheleth* says, "be happy; but when times are bad, consider: God has made the one as well as the other. Therefore, a man cannot discover anything about his future."[168] Don't quite know everything, do you?

"I have seen . . . a righteous man perishing in his righteousness, and a wicked man living long in his wickedness,"[169] he says. You have, too. Have you figured it out? Didn't think so. Don't quite know everything, do you?

He goes on,

Do not be overrighteous,
    neither be overwise—
    why destroy yourself?
Do not be overwicked,
    and do not be a fool—
    why die before your time?
It is good to grasp the one
    and not let go of the other.
    Whoever who fears God will avoid all extremes.[170]

Can you believe that? The Bible telling you not to be "overrighteous?" No? Didn't even know that was a word? Don't quite know everything, do you?[171]

"Wisdom makes one wise man more powerful than ten rulers in a city," he writes. And then, "There is not a righteous man on earth who does what is right and never sins."[172] Then, in case you are tempted to argue with that last line:

Do not pay attention to every word people say,
    or you may hear your servant cursing you—
for you know in your heart
    that many times you yourself have cursed others.[173]

"All this I tested by wisdom," he continues, "and I said, 'I am determined to be wise'—but this was beyond me.'"[174] Don't quite know everything, do you?

"Whatever wisdom may be, it is far off and most profound—who can discover it?"[175] Yup. Don't quite know everything.

"So I turned my mind to understand, to investigate and to search out wisdom and the scheme of things and to understand the stupidity of wickedness and the madness of folly."[176] Is that so, *Qoheleth*? I thought you already said as much back in chapter 1. But, okay, what did you find out about the stupidity of wickedness and the madness of folly? He answers:

> I find more bitter than death
>> the woman who is a snare,
> whose heart is a trap
>> and whose hands are chains.
> The man who pleases God will escape her,
>> but the sinner she will ensnare.

"Look," says the Teacher, "this is what I have discovered:

"Adding one thing to another to discover the scheme of things—
>> while I was still searching
>> but not finding—
> I found one upright man among a thousand,
>> but not one upright woman among them all.[177]
> This only have I found:
>> God made mankind upright,
>> but men have gone in search of many schemes."[178]

As wise as we might be (or might think we are), *Qoheleth's* earlier question remains:

> Who can straighten
> what [God] has made crooked?[179]

Or, as the New Living Translation puts it,

> Accept the way God does things;
> for who can straighten what he has made crooked?[180]

So why does my life have to be so hard, when yours is a piece of cake? "Who can straighten what [God] has made crooked?"

Why does my very own daughter, my firstborn, the apple of my eye, listen to country music? "Who can straighten what [God] has made crooked?"

Why are Bigfoot and the Loch Ness Monster so camera shy? "Who can straighten what [God] has made crooked?"

The questions can go on forever. But it is far better to do as Solomon advises in his collection of proverbs:

> Trust in the LORD with all your heart
>> and lean not on your own understanding;
> in all your ways acknowledge him,
>> and he will make your paths straight.[181]

Don't lean on your own understanding. Don't trust your own intelligence. Don't rely solely on human wisdom. Trust explicitly in God's wisdom.

Do Acquire All the Wisdom You Can

Ecclesiastes 8:1 asks another question, which suggests another "do" to us:

> Who is like the wise?
>> Who knows the explanation of things?
> A person's wisdom brightens their face
>> and changes its hard appearance.[182]

Once again, the New Living Translation takes a helpful slant in translating the first phrase of that verse:

> How wonderful to be wise,
>> to analyze and interpret things.[183]

But how? That's the question. How do I acquire that kind of wisdom? How can I get wiser as I get older ? How do I get to the point of being able to analyze and interpret things?

It's not an easy question to answer, but let me offer a few suggestions that I think are in keeping with *Qoheleth's* perspective.

1. Seek God. The Bible says—repeatedly, in fact—

> How does a man become wise?
> The first step is to trust and reverence the Lord![184]

I promise you, if you seek God wholeheartedly, if you worship him daily, if you make *him* your focus, your priority, if you listen to him, pray and read his Word, seek to please him in all you do, you will become wiser than you ever thought you could. It may not be an easy road. It may not happen at the pace you'd like. It may involve more than a few lessons learned the hard way. But day by day, year by year, trusting and reverencing the Lord will make you wiser than you could ever be otherwise. (Get it? "Other-wise?" It's clever, take my word for it.)

2. Ask God. God's Word says,

> If any of you lacks wisdom. . . .

Let's pause for just a moment there. If you've ever doubted that God has a sense of humor, doubt no more. That verse I just started quoting is proof positive. It is one of the funniest verses in the Bible, though few people ever recognize it as such. But think about it. James 1:5 begins,

> *If* any of you lacks wisdom. . . .

"IF!" What a hoot! *If* any of you lacks wisdom! As if there's any question, any doubt. As if there is a single man or woman among us who *doesn't* lack wisdom. Comedy gold. But it goes on from there to say:

> If any of you lacks wisdom, he should ask God.[185]

As Solomon did. When God gave King David's son and successor carte blanche to ask for anything—anything at all—he asked for wisdom. And so should we all. Whatever *other* needs we may have, we should ask God for wisdom.

It is amazing that we God-lovers and Christ-followers, who know the story of Solomon and have read and heard about God's favorable and generous reaction to Solomon's request for wisdom, nonetheless go through our daily lives asking for health, financial blessings, protection from speeding tickets, and deliverance from threatened layoffs while routinely, habitually neglecting to ask for wisdom. It ought to be one of our first thoughts whenever we do something or go somewhere. It ought to be a daily request. It ought to be one of the most frequent cries we make to God.

3. Follow godly counsel. Proverbs 12:15 says,

> Fools are headstrong and do what they like;
> wise people take advice."[186]

I can't tell you how many times in my experience as a pastor people have said to me and to others, "Thanks, Pastor, but...." I can't tell you how many people I've watched who let godly counsel go in one ear and out the other. I can't tell you how many people have made train wrecks of their lives by avoiding or ignoring godly counsel.

The Bible also says, "There is safety in having many advisors."[187] I've seen people who made unwise decisions because they leaned exclusively on one person for counsel and guidance. Though that person was upright and well intentioned, he or she lacked the experience that a larger circle of advisors could have provided.

Of course, often when you seek counsel from multiple sources, you'll receive conflicting ideas. You'll have to weigh one suggestion against another. It can be downright difficult and confusing. But if you don't ask, or if you *do* ask, and the wisest, godliest people in your life are telling you mostly the same thing, you're a fool not to take their advice. And the flip side of that is, you'll grow in wisdom and learn from wise, godly counsel even when you make a mistake. The experience itself will teach you volumes and deepen your capacity for wisdom.

4. Study to acquire wisdom. The Bible says, "Wise men store up knowledge."[188] Storing up knowledge is a different process from, say, watching television or cruising the Internet. Passive pursuits like watching YouTube videos or playing Words with Friends don't store up knowledge. To do that takes action: reading, thinking, discussing, writing, and reflecting.

In fact, even listening to good preaching is too often a passive activity in today's churches (or, worse, via television, radio, or podcast). If you want to store up knowledge, you must interact with thoughts, facts, and words. Take notes. Highlight. Outline. Cross-reference. Ask questions. Debate. Discuss.

Take the time to read God's Word, but do more than that. Interact with it. Memorize it. Study it. Pray it.

Become familiar with wisdom literature, like Proverbs, Ecclesiastes, and Job.

Don't just make mistakes, reflect on them, learn from them, and maybe write down what you learned.

Don't just curse your luck when life stinks, but allow God to teach you wisdom through your trials.

From time to time, turn OFF the radio in the car and think through—or pray through—areas where you need to acquire more wisdom.

John Maxwell, in his book, *Thinking for a Change*, suggests many good ideas for thinking and developing the life of the mind. One of them is that of devoting a specific place and time to thinking through things, much as you might designate a place and time for prayer and Bible reading. He says he spends most of his time thinking in three places: the car, planes, and in his backyard hot tub.[189] His success as an author and leadership expert may have something to do with intentionally making time and devoting space to the thinking process.

5. Hang out with wise people. Another of Solomon's many proverbs says,

> Practice God's law—get a reputation for wisdom;
> hang out with a loose crowd—embarrass your family.[190]

In other words, don't hang around with ninnies; spend time with wise people, observe how they conduct themselves, how they think through a matter, when they speak and when they're silent, and so on. Some of it might rub off, and some of it you'll have to learn more purposefully.

When I first began dating the lovely Robin, the woman who became my wife, I seemed to many an unpromising young man. My mother had died in my early teens; my older brothers were both grown and out of the house. I had the barest of social graces and knew nothing about how to treat a young woman. But I was fortunate to have wise and patient friends of both sexes, and I learned a little from talking to and watching them. I had a couple surrogate "big sisters" who took me under their wings and coached me. And, most importantly—and inexplicably—I learned from Robin herself who, in the early weeks and months of our relationship, patiently schooled me in how she expected and preferred to be treated. She was—and still is—to me the wisest and loveliest of counselors a man could have, and the time I spent with her was not only romantically intoxicating but also intellectually stimulating, socially edifying, and spiritually enriching.

Wise people hang out with wise people. "Walk with the wise and become wise," as Solomon said, "for a companion of fools suffers harm."[191]

Do Exercise Humility and Wisdom Together

In Ecclesiastes 8:2–15, *Qoheleth* revisits many of his previous themes. He says, basically, "Be a good citizen" (vv. 2–5), "Be aware of your mortality" (vv. 6–8), "Be realistic about injustice" (vv. 9–14), "Be content to eat, drink, and enjoy life" (v. 15), after which he offers a concluding thought to his ruminations on the limits of human wisdom:

> When I applied my mind to know wisdom and to observe
> the labor that is done on earth—people getting no sleep
> day or night—then I saw all that God has done. No one
> can comprehend what goes on under the sun. Despite all
> their efforts to search it out, no one can discover its mean-
> ing. Even if the wise claim they know, they cannot really
> comprehend it.[192]

Here's the thing: the moment you congratulate yourself for your wisdom, the moment you declare yourself to be wise—that's the moment you cease to be wise. As Mahatma Gandhi said, "It is unwise to be too sure of one's own wisdom."[193]

And the Bible actually makes it clear that humility and wisdom are inextricably linked; the one comes from the other. James wrote,

> Who is wise and understanding among you? Let them
> show it by their good life, by deeds done in the humility
> that comes from wisdom.[194]

You see, most of us have a rather prideful attitude that says, "I oughta be able to understand everything that goes on around me." It's as if we say to God, "Hey! I need to be in the loop, you know!" It's not so much that we think God needs to consult us, but he should definitely update us, you know? Keep us posted. Explain himself to us. And maybe give fair warning when he's going to do something strange or dangerous. But *Qoheleth* says,

> Accept the way God does things;
>> for who can straighten what he has made crooked?[195]

Much of our stress and dissatisfaction in life springs from trying to straighten what God has made crooked—or trying to bend what he has made straight. We have our own ideas about how things ought to go, and we're seldom shy about telling him, often in great detail, what he should do. But his ways are not our ways. His ways are so much higher than our ways that we can't even make out the lower limits of his wisdom.

If we are wise, we will be humble. We will remind ourselves that he knows what is best. We will seek him, first and foremost. We will tell him where and how much we lack wisdom and ask him to supply our need, first and foremost through his presence, his Word, and his voice in our hearts and also by means of the counsel of godly people. We will study to acquire greater wisdom and, when he provides, do our best to exercise wisdom and humility together.

———— ❧ ————

Lord God, your Word says, "If any of you lacks wisdom, he should ask God."[196] So I ask. Please give me your wisdom. Give me the wisdom to seek you every day. Give me the wisdom to recognize and accept the way you do things. Give me wisdom in my daily life, in how I conduct my life, in the habits and routines I observe. Give me wisdom in my relationships with my loved ones and my friends, with neighbors and co-workers. Give me wisdom in my work, my finances, and my household. Give me wisdom as I pray and read your Word. Give me wisdom as I worship and serve you in the church. Give me wisdom through trials and temptations. Give me the wisdom to "walk with the wise."[197] Give me the wisdom to be humble, and to acquire more wisdom. In Jesus' name, amen.

LIVE EVERY DAY
AS IF IT'S YOUR LAST;
SOMEDAY YOU'LL BE RIGHT

I learned a new word recently. A friend from church sent me an email of paraprosdokians. These are figures of speech in which the latter part of a phrase or sentence is surprising in a way that prompts a new understanding—even contradiction—of the first part. Paraprosdokians were a favorite rhetorical device of Will Rogers ("I don't belong to an organized political party. I'm a Democrat"), Groucho Marx ("I've had a perfectly wonderful evening, but this wasn't it"), Winston Churchill ("You can always count on the Americans to do the right thing—after they have tried everything else"), and comedian Steven Wright ("The last thing I want to do is hurt you; but it's still on the list").

Though I didn't have a word for it until now, I've enjoyed paraprosdokians for years. Some of my personal favorites are these:

I'd really like to agree with you, but then we'd both be
wrong.

We never really grow up; we only learn how to act in
public.

War does not determine who is right, only who is left.

Knowledge is knowing a tomato is a fruit. Wisdom is not
putting it in a fruit salad.

To steal ideas from one person is plagiarism. To steal from
many is research.

I didn't say it was your fault, I said I was blaming you.

Women will never be equal to men until they can walk
down the street with a bald head and a beer gut, and
still think they are sexy.

You do not need a parachute to skydive. You only need a
parachute to skydive twice.

You're never too old to learn something stupid.

I asked God for a bike, but I know God doesn't work that
way. So I stole a bike and asked for forgiveness.

A bus station is where a bus stops. A train station is where
a train stops. On my desk, I have a work station.

One careless match can start a forest fire, but it takes a
whole box to start a campfire.

Some people are like Slinkies—not really good for
anything, but you can't help smiling when you see one
tumble down the stairs.

A clear conscience is usually the sign of a bad memory.

The voices in my head may not be real, but they have some
good ideas!

Always borrow money from a pessimist. He won't expect
it back.

The author of Ecclesiastes may not have known the word *parapros-dokian* (it is based on Greek words meaning, "against expectations"), but something tells me he would have been a fan. After all, in the first eight chapters of his treatise on the value and meaning of life, *Qoheleth* has already spouted such paraprosdokians (or near-para-prosdokians) as these:

> I have seen the burden God has laid on the human race. He has made everything beautiful in its time.[198]

> [God] has . . . set eternity in the human heart; yet no one can fathom what God has done from beginning to end.[199]

> As goods increase, so do those who consume them.[200]

> Everyone's toil is for their mouth, yet their appetite is never satisfied.[201]

> The more the words, the less the meaning.[202]

> Death is the destiny of everyone; the living should take this to heart[203] (as if the dead *could*!).

These may not be the best examples of paraprosdokians, but they do seem to capture the ironic and whimsical spirit of the form. In fact, the entire book of Ecclesiastes (which, by the way, warns against the futility of writing books![204]) can be seen as a sort of long-form paraprosdokian that says, "Here's some wisdom for you: wisdom is meaningless." Or, as philosopher Jacques Ellul put it, "The only true wisdom we can aspire to consists of the perception that no wisdom is possible."[205]

Life Is Hard, but at Least It's Short

The paraprosdokian quality of Ecclesiastes certainly holds true as the ninth chapter begins, and *Qoheleth* begins steering toward a conclusion. The first ten verses of that chapter, which could be titled, "Life Is Hard, but at Least It's Short," offer a blunt assessment of life (and death) and four practical responses to the common mortality we all share.

Live with the End in Mind

Even after writing roughly 3,700 words about the meaning (or meaninglessness) of life, *Qoheleth* still has a lot of wisdom to share. He has explored money, power, pleasure, education, justice, popularity, wisdom, and more and is still only about 70 percent of the way to his finale. But he makes it clear, as Ecclesiastes 9 begins, that he is moving in that direction:

> So I reflected on all this and concluded that the righteous and the wise and what they do are in God's hands, but no one knows whether love or hate awaits them. All share a common destiny—the righteous and the wicked, the good and the bad, the clean and the unclean, those who offer sacrifices and those who do not.
>
> As it is with the good,
>   so with the sinful;
> as it is with those who take oaths,
>   so with those who are afraid to take them.
>
> This is the evil in everything that happens under the sun: The same destiny overtakes all. The hearts of people, moreover, are full of evil and there is madness in their hearts while they live, and afterward they join the dead. Anyone who is among the living has hope—even a live dog is better off than a dead lion!
>
> For the living know that they will die,

> but the dead know nothing;
> they have no further reward,
>   and even their name is forgotten.
> Their love, their hate
>   and their jealousy have long since vanished;
> never again will they have a part
>   in anything that happens under the sun.[206]

When *Qoheleth* says, "The same destiny overtakes all,"[207] he is not espousing universalism, the belief that everyone will end up in paradise sooner or later. He is saying that death awaits us all. That is truth. That is reality. It is a blunt, practical, accurate assessment of life: it ends for everyone.

That means, of course, that it will end for you. Maybe today. Maybe many years from today. But everyone— the righteous and the wicked, the good and the bad, the clean and the unclean, those who offer sacrifices and those who do not—are living on borrowed time. And it is wise not only to confront that reality about your future but also to let it shape your future. It is prudent and practical to live with the end in mind.

Stephen Covey, in his acclaimed book *The Seven Habits of Highly Effective People*, made this principle the second of his transforming and empowering "habits." He wrote:

> In your mind's eye, see yourself going to the funeral of a
> loved one. Picture yourself driving to the funeral parlor
> or chapel, parking the car, and getting out. As you walk
> inside the building, you notice the flowers, the soft organ
> music. You see the faces of friends and family you pass
> along the way. You feel the shared sorrow of losing, the
> joy of having known, that radiates from the hearts of the
> people there.

As you walk down to the front of the room and look inside the casket, you suddenly come face to face with yourself. This is your funeral, three years from today. All these people have come to honor you, to express feelings of love and appreciation for your life.

As you take a seat and wait for the services to begin, you look at the program in your hand. There are to be four speakers. The first is from your family, immediate and also extended—children, brothers, sisters, nephews, nieces, aunts, uncles, cousins, and grandparents who have come from all over the country to attend. The second speaker is one of your friends, someone who can give a sense of what you were as a person. The third speaker is from your work or profession. And the fourth is from your church or some community organization where you've been involved in service.

Now think deeply. What would you like each of these speakers to say about you and your life? What kind of husband, wife, father, or mother would you like their words to reflect? What kind of son or daughter or cousin? What kind of friend? What kind of working associate?

What character would you like them to have seen in you? What contributions, what achievements would you want them to remember? Look carefully at the people around you. What difference would you like to have made in their lives?[208]

Whether you are young or old, "righteous" or "wicked," universally loved or generally despised, "The day will come when somebody tries to sum you up,"[209] says Frederick Buechner. That is why *Qoheleth* and Covey advise you to live with the end in mind. There will come a day when your love, hate, and jealousy have long since vanished, and you will never again have a part in anything that happens under the sun—but that day is not yet. "Anyone who is among the living has hope,"[210] *Qoheleth* says, and there is every reason to begin now, this moment, while there is hope, to live with the end—your end—in mind.

Years ago, I decided to plan my own funeral. My reason at the time was to save my wife and children from the stress of having to come up with a service outline if I were to precede them in death. But the exercise also prompted some valuable reflection, not only about what I'd like my funeral to be like, but also about what I want the rest of my life to be like.

It could do the same for you. Are there things you're holding onto that you'd be sorry about at the end of your life? Are there things you'd wish you had said? Tried? Accomplished? Forgiven? If you are among the living (and you *must be*, if you're reading these words), then there is hope. Start living with the end in mind.

Live—Now!—With Relish

Death is unavoidable, *Qoheleth* says. It will come to us all (Bible scholar Alphonse Maillot originally titled his commentary on Ecclesiastes, *Brothers, We Must Die*[211]). But that doesn't mean we should hunker down and await the inevitable. On the contrary, he says:

> Go, eat your food with gladness, and drink your wine with a joyful heart, for God has already approved what you do. Always be clothed in white, and always anoint your head with oil.[212]

That first word of verse 7, "Go," is only two letters in English, but it is a big word nonetheless. It could be capitalized or italicized. In my personal study Bible, it is both underlined and circled. *Qoheleth* is saying, "Get up! Get to it! Time's wasting!" *The Message* paraphrase renders it "Seize life!"[213] Warren W. Wiersbe interprets it, "Don't sit around and brood! Get up and live!"[214]

The reality and universality of death, *Qoheleth* says, is all the more reason to live your life with relish, with gusto. The brevity of life makes it all the more precious. The frailty of life makes it even more urgent to eat your food with gladness and drink your wine with a joyful heart. Enjoy every bite. Savor every swallow, "for God has already approved what you do"[215]—or, to quote *The Message* again, "God takes pleasure in *your* pleasure!"[216]

Have you ever given a gift to a child—your son or daughter, perhaps, or a grandchild—and been so excited to see that child enjoy your gift? At my granddaughter Calleigh's second birthday celebration, once she understood that all the presents in the room were intended for her, she settled into a pattern. She would open a package to see what was inside, then set it down on the floor by her chair and announce, "Next!" Her imperious manner made us all laugh, but it was a tad disappointing, nonetheless, for my wife and I to see her treat *our* gift so glibly; we wanted her to rejoice and revel in the gift we had so carefully chosen for her. Similarly, God has given you the life you have, for however long you have it; surely he wants to see you enjoying his gift. He takes pleasure in *your* pleasure.

The emotional climax of Thornton Wilder's classic play, *Our Town*, takes place in Act 3, when Emily, who died giving birth to her second child, says farewell to life:

> Good-by, good-by, world. Good-by, Grover's Corners
> . . . Mama and Papa. Good-by to clocks ticking . . . and
> Mama's sunflowers. And food and coffee. And new-ironed
> dresses and hot baths . . . and sleeping and waking up. Oh,
> earth, you're too wonderful for anybody to realize you. Did
> any human beings ever realize life (and how wonderful it
> is) while they live it? Every, every minute.[217]

"If one accepts each day as a gift from the Father's hand," writes Gerhard Frost, "one may sometimes hear a voice saying, 'Open it . . . unwrap the hidden beauties in an ordinary day.'"[218] So, *Qoheleth* says, "Always be clothed in white, and always anoint your head with oil."[219] The emphasis in these two phrases of verse 8 is on the word, "always." It was the custom of the day to wear white robes only on holidays and anoint your head with fragrant oils at banquets. Such luxuries were reserved for special occasions. But *Qoheleth* says, "Don't wait for a special occasion. *Always* be clothed in white. *Always* anoint your head with oil." In our day and age, he might say, "Don't wait for a special occasion to use the good china. You shouldn't need an excuse to wear your best clothes. Go ahead, pamper yourself. *Every* day is a special occasion! Live it up! Have some fun! Grab the gusto!"

Life is too short to approach it any other way. As author Tim Hansel wrote:

> Don't be bashful.
>> Bite in.
> Pick it up with your fingers and
>> let the juice that may
>>> roll down your chin.
>
> Life is ready and ripe.
>> NOW
>>> whenever you are.
>
> You don't need a knife or fork
> or spoon or napkin or tablecloth
>
> For there is no core
>> or stem
>> or rind
>> or pit

> or seed
> or skin
>   to throw away.[220]

Prioritize the People in Your Life

Qoheleth's next words echo the beautiful counsel Solomon offered in one of his proverbs, in which he said to "rejoice in the wife of your youth"[221]:

> Enjoy life with your wife, whom you love, all the days of
> this meaningless life that God has given you under the
> sun—all your meaningless days. For this is your lot in life
> and in your toilsome labor under the sun.[222]

The New Living Translation phrases this verse a little differently:

> Live happily with the woman you love through all the
> meaningless days of life that God has given you under the
> sun. The wife God gives you is your reward for all your
> earthly toil.[223]

He is writing, of course, from a man's perspective, to a predominantly male audience, so it is unsurprising that he talks about enjoying life with your wife (rather than "husband or wife," or "spouse," as we might phrase it today). What is somewhat surprising, however, is his focus on "wife"—not wives. Remember, King Solomon had hundreds of wives and concubines. Yet, as he heads toward a conclusion, he seems to acknowledge that there is a singular joy to be found in a strong, loving, exclusive relationship between a husband and wife.

When I preside over a wedding, one of my favorite moments in the sacred ceremony is when I ask the bride and groom to face each other and hold hands. I tell them to forget that anyone else is present and look into each other's eyes. Then, after a moment, I will say to them, "*This* . . . is how much God loves you." Sometimes I can barely get out the words because the thought chokes me up every time, invested as it is with my awareness of the great reward *my* wife is to me. The wife—or husband—God gives you is a huge blessing, and you can do no better than to "Live happily with the woman you love through all the meaningless days of life that God has given you."[224]

But it is possible to extend *Qoheleth*'s wise words a little further. As he writes about the brevity of life and the wisdom of enjoying it as much as possible for as long as possible, he turns unavoidably to the value of relationships—which we can and should apply not only to the marriage bond but to all of the people in our lives.

If you aspire to live well even in the midst of a sick world, you will make a priority of the people in your life, and the most important people in your life will assume the highest priority. Thinking back to Stephen Covey's "funeral parlor" exercise, who are the people you picture in that room? Who do you most want to be there? Who would you want to speak? Those are the people who should be taking the top slots in your list of priorities.

Are they?

Or do your daily calendar and to-do list reflect different priorities? Is your time—your life—being spent on other things? Are you spending the best parts of your life with the wife whom you love or with the job you worked so hard to get? Or the boat you're still making payments on? Or the habit you just can't quit? How much better would it be to:

Enjoy life with your wife or husband, whom you love . . .
Enjoy life with your children, whom you love . . .
Enjoy life with your grandchildren, whom you love . . .
Enjoy life with your parents, whom you love . . .
Enjoy life with your siblings, whom you love . . .
Enjoy life with your nieces and nephews, whom you love . . .

Enjoy life with your good friends, whom you love . . .

Enjoy life with your church family, small group, and favorite co-workers, whom you love . . .

Enjoy life with the people you love, through all the meaningless days of life that God has given you under the sun. They are your reward for all your earthly toil.

Make the Most of Every Moment, Every Breath

Qoheleth closes this section of his treatise with a bang. He writes,

> Whatever your hand finds to do, do it with all your might,
> for in the realm of the dead, where you are going, there
> is neither working nor planning nor knowledge nor
> wisdom.[225]

The Apostle Paul may have had Ecclesiastes in mind when he challenged the early Christians in Colosse:

> Whatever you do, work at it with all your heart, as work-
> ing for the Lord, not for human masters.[226]

Both *Qoheleth* and Paul prescribe a wholehearted embracing, a full-throttle pursuit of life while it lasts. It is the same spirit espoused by Henry David Thoreau in his Walden experiment:

> I wanted to live deep and suck out all the marrow of life,
> to live so sturdily and Spartan-like as to put to rout all that
> was not life, to cut a broad swath and shave close, to drive
> life into a corner, and reduce it to its lowest terms, and, if it
> proved to be mean, why then to get the whole and genuine
> meanness of it, and publish its meanness to the world; or
> if it were sublime, to know it by experience, and be able to
> give a true account of it in my next excursion.[227]

Live deep, *Qoheleth* says. Don't just nibble at the edges; suck out all the marrow of life. Don't stare at the ground and shuffle your feet; grab life with both hands and spin it around the dance floor. Don't hold back; dive in. Don't wait for the weather to change; splash in the puddles. Give *this* day, *this* moment, *this* breath, all you've got, because you don't know how much of it you've got left.

Qoheleth would have found a kindred spirit in American humorist Erma Bombeck, who in 1979 wrote the following in her syndicated newspaper column:

> If I had my life to live over again I would have waxed less and listened more.
>
> Instead of wishing away nine months of pregnancy and complaining about the shadow over my feet, I'd have cherished every minute of it and realized that the wonderment growing inside me was to be my only chance in life to assist God in a miracle.
>
> I would never have insisted the car windows be rolled up on a summer day because my hair had just been teased and sprayed.
>
> I would have invited friends over to dinner even if the carpet was stained and the sofa faded.
>
> I would have eaten popcorn in the "good" living room and worried less about the dirt when you lit the fireplace.
>
> I would have taken the time to listen to my grandfather ramble about his youth.
>
> I would have burnt the pink candle that was sculptured like a rose before it melted while being stored.
>
> I would have sat cross-legged on the lawn with my children and never worried about grass stains.
>
> I would have cried and laughed less while watching television . . . and more while watching real life.

I would have shared more of the responsibility carried by my husband which I took for granted.

I would have eaten less cottage cheese and more ice cream.

I would have gone to bed when I was sick, instead of pretending the Earth would go into a holding pattern if I weren't there for a day.

I would never have bought ANYTHING just because it was practical/wouldn't show soil/guaranteed to last a lifetime.

When my child kissed me impetuously, I would never have said, "Later. Now, go get washed up for dinner."

There would have been more I love yous . . . more I'm sorrys . . . more I'm listenings . . . but mostly, given another shot at life, I would seize every minute of it . . . look at it and really see it . . . try it on . . . live it . . . exhaust it . . . and never give that minute back until there was nothing left of it.[228]

The Jerusalem Talmud, a commentary on the Hebrew Scriptures collected in the fourth and fifth centuries, says, "In the world to come, a man will have to give an accounting for every good thing his eyes saw, but of which he did not eat."[229] How many good things has God given you that you have not eaten? How many days has he given that you have not fully enjoyed? How many minutes? How many breaths? Snatch every good thing God has given you and squeeze the juice out of it.

Seize every minute of your life. *Exhaust* it, as Bombeck said. Suck the marrow out of it, like Thoreau, until it has given you all it has to give. And then, like Oliver Twist tiptoeing to the master's table with basin and spoon in hand, extend your arms and say, "Please, sir, I want some more."[230]

———————— ∿ ————————

Heavenly Father, I want to take a few moments to meditate in your presence and ask you to speak to me.

Are there things I'm holding onto that I'd be sorry about at the end of my life?

Are there things I will wish I had said?

Things I will wish I had tried?

Accomplished?

Forgiven?

Speak, Lord, and help me to hear you clearly and respond fully to whatever you say. I want to live the rest of my life with the end in mind. I ask you to help me shape my future so that I will have no regrets when this life is over. I want to seize life. I want to accept each day as a gift from your hand, treating it as the special occasion that it is. I want to prioritize the people in my life and enjoy life with them for as long as I live. I want to "live deep and suck out all the marrow of life."[231] I want to grab life with both hands and spin it around the dance floor. I want to splash in the puddles. I want to give this day, this moment, this breath all I've got, for as long as I've got. Help me, Lord. In Jesus' name, amen.

LIFE IS LIKE A BOX OF CHOCOLATES; IT CAN BE SWEET, BUT IT CAN MAKE YOU SICK, TOO

I had heard of cystic fibrosis. But I knew next to nothing about it.

My third grandchild had just been born, the first child of my daughter and her husband. They named her Calleigh. She bounced into the world looking healthy in every way, at seven pounds and thirteen ounces. Every test the hospital performed returned positive results. She was wrapped in a pink blanket and sent home.

But soon, concerns arose. I'll let my daughter Aubrey, Calleigh's mother, tell the rest:

> We spent those first few weeks trying everything we could—breastfeeding, experimenting with different formulas, etc.—in order to get Calleigh to gain weight. My husband Kevin and I were so wrapped up in being a new mommy and daddy and figuring things out (and I was

wrapped up in a lot of post-pregnancy hormones) that we
didn't realize how skinny she had gotten; it took looking
back at pictures to see it. But she seemed to be constantly
hungry. She would eat and eat but not gain weight, and
her digestion seemed painful to her at times.

After a couple weeks, the doctors told us that
Calleigh's newborn screening had shown an abnormality.
They said she needed more tests. They explained that
one possible reason for the results was cystic fibrosis, a
genetic disease that causes thick, sticky mucus to build up
in the lungs, digestive tract, and other areas of the body,
resulting in life-threatening lung infections and serious
digestion problems. They said a sweat test would confirm
or eliminate that possibility. So at just a few weeks old,
Calleigh was taken to the hospital, where they wrapped
her in layers of warm clothing to try to get her to produce
enough sweat for the test. Even then, it didn't seem real.
We couldn't imagine that anything could be so seriously
wrong with our precious, perfect daughter.

I was alone at home when the doctor's office called
with the test results. They offered me the choice of finding
out over the phone or coming in to hear the news. I braced
myself; surely if the news was good, they wouldn't have
to give me a choice. The voice on the phone confirmed
what I had refused to imagine. Calleigh had cystic fibrosis.
Somehow I held it together long enough to thank them
and hang up. I called my parents, dialing the phone with
shaking hands.

"I need you," I said.

They were in the car, headed somewhere, but they
turned around and drove to my house. Kevin was at work,

and I didn't want him to hear the news over the phone,
so I sat down beside Calleigh's bed and let the tears flow
while I stared at her. I didn't pick her up; I worried that she
would sense my pain and panic.

At some point, my parents arrived and my father took
Calleigh while I cried in my mother's arms. When Kevin
got home from work, Mom and Dad took Calleigh into
the next room so I could tell him the news—though he
didn't need to hear the words. He knew the moment he
saw my face. We held each other and cried together, griev-
ing the loss of the perfect health our daughter never had.

You've probably endured something like that. In fact, you may have
suffered worse. Many people have.

The boss called you in. Talked about what a fine job you've been
doing. Called you an asset to the company. After the words, "cut-
backs" and "layoffs," you more or less zoned out. You'd heard enough.
Enough to be scared.

The doctor called. The results of those routine tests turned out
to be not so routine. The news could be worse, but it could be a whole
lot better.

The phone rings. "There's been an accident."

A note from school, asking for a meeting.

A knock on the door. *Why would the police be here?*

Moments like that can change your life. They can be devastat-
ing. They can make you or break you; they can even do both. Some
people are fond of saying, "What doesn't kill you makes you stronger."
That's not always true. Sometimes what doesn't kill you knocks you
senseless. Sometimes what doesn't kill you disables you, if only for a
time. Sometimes what doesn't kill you maims you. Sometimes what
doesn't kill you hurts you so deeply, you can't go on.

That's one of the ways life stinks. It can be cruel. Heartless. Utterly and unrelentingly hard.

John, one of Jesus' closest friends, recorded an incident in Jesus' life. One day Jesus and his disciples came upon a man who had been born blind. John says, "His disciples asked him, 'Rabbi, who sinned, this man or his parents, that he was born blind?'"[232] It's interesting that John didn't specify who did the asking. We may assume that the twelve disciples didn't all speak at once, in unison. A couple of them may have wondered aloud and persuaded one of them to speak up. Maybe John masked the identity of the questioner because it was a stupid question; no one likes to look stupid (especially if it's going to be mentioned in the Bible!). Or maybe he doesn't say who asked the question because it was so rude to say such a thing in the man's hearing; after all, though John doesn't specifically say that the man heard the question, later verses do reveal that, while the man was blind, he wasn't deaf! Or maybe it was just that when John went to record the event he couldn't be sure who asked the question.

But think about it. The question assumed that the man was blind because either he or his parents had sinned. Something was wrong, they reasoned, therefore someone had *done* wrong. But remember, the man was *born* blind. Was it possible that he had sinned *in the womb?* What could he have done to deserve blindness from birth? It boggles the mind.

Unfortunately, however, that is still all too common. When something terrible happens, don't we often respond, "What did I do to deserve this?" When children stray, don't we ask, "What did I do wrong?" When tragedy hits, don't we tend to think in terms of, "If only I had left a little earlier or taken a different route"?

But Jesus' answer to his disciples' question about whether the man's sin or his parents' sin had caused his blindness was, "Neither!" He dispelled the notion that the man's blindness was a punishment for sin. In fact, he went further than that. He said the man's blindness—rather than being a curse—was an opportunity. The circumstances that had made him a beggar could be turned around and result in God's glory.

And the same can happen in my life and yours. As hard as life can be at times, it is possible to live well through it all—as Ecclesiastes shows us.

Forrest Gump Was Right

A single white feather floats on the breeze. Above treetops and housetops. Past church steeples and pillared porticoes. Falling and rising, as a whimsical piano melody plays. Soaring and spinning, almost alighting on a man's shoulder as he waits at a crosswalk, until it finally rests against a dirty tennis shoe worn by a man seated on a bench at a bus stop. The man picks it up, inspects it, and then opens the small, neatly packed suitcase on the bench beside him and tucks the feather between the pages of a book.

Soon a bus comes and goes, but the man stays seated. He picks up a box of chocolates and opens it. A woman sits on the other end of the bench. He introduces himself and, though she doesn't respond, he extends the box in her direction and asks if she wants a chocolate. Then he adds, "My momma always said life was like a box of chocolates—you never know what you're gonna get."

You probably recognize that as the opening scene from the hugely popular (and award-winning) movie, *Forrest Gump*, based on Winston Groom's novel of the same name.[233] And you've almost certainly heard or seen Forrest's words (though usually quoted as "Life *is* like a box of chocolates") repeated numerous times. That famous aphorism has become part of our modern lexicon. It's cute. It's quaint. And it happens to be true.

Of course, that's far from the only way life is like a box of chocolates. Some others are these:

> Life is like a box of chocolates: you have to poke around to get what you want.
> Life is like a box of chocolates: you're probably not gonna like every little piece.
> Life is like a box of chocolates: it's much less appealing in 100-degree heat.
> Life is like a box of chocolates: somebody always gets to the best pieces before you do.
> Life is like a box of chocolates: it's better with a good cup of coffee.
> Life is like a box of chocolates: A cheap, thoughtless, perfunctory gift that nobody ever asks for.[234]

The author of Ecclesiastes probably would have agreed with most of those thoughts. Life is like a box of chocolates in a lot of ways—but especially because you never know what you're going to get, even if (as in some boxes of assorted chocolates) the contents are printed right inside the box top. In the case of Ecclesiastes, contents for life appear in all its pages, though they may not always be obvious or easy to discern. But they are there, nonetheless. In fact, in the ninth and tenth chapters of his treatise, *Qoheleth* offers four hugely valuable instructions for living well in a sick world, in spite of life's unpredictability.

Learn to Expect the Unexpected

The day I began this chapter, I was already a few days behind in my writing schedule. My deadline was looming. I was feeling the pressure big time.

I'm not complaining—I love being a writer—but one of the exigencies of the working writer's life is that not only is there always a deadline hanging over your head like a Damoclean sword, but there is almost always another deadline after that. And maybe another still beyond *that* one. That's a good thing, believe me, because a writer without deadlines is likely to be a writer without income. But it has its downside, too, because failure to meet your deadline makes the next one that much harder to meet. And so on, like a row of falling dominoes.

So it wasn't as if I didn't have enough to worry about. But then I received an email from an editor. Attached to the email was the edited manuscript of my next book, due to be released in less than two months. It was my job to review those hundreds of edits, questions, and comments from the editor and respond to them within a week—a task that wouldn't have been a problem if I weren't already staring down the deadline on this book.

That day I received a second email. From a different editor. Of another book. Attached to that email was the edited manuscript of one more book, one that was due for release in seven months. A response to those edits was needed in just a few days.

Did I mention that I was already on deadline? That I was already behind? That I needed more time, not more to do?

I realize my plight may not evoke much sympathy. As I said, I love being a writer. And there are much worse adversities that could crowd into my life. I realize that. But whether the interruptions are big or small, catastrophic or merely irritating, few of us like it when the unexpected happens. We want life to be smooth, predictable, comfy, and cozy. But *Qoheleth* advises us to learn to expect the unexpected:

I have seen something else under the sun:

The race is not to the swift

> or the battle to the strong,
> nor does food come to the wise
> or wealth to the brilliant
> or favor to the learned;
> but time and chance happen to them all.[235]

In Hebrew, unlike English, a writer has the option of changing the emphasis in a sentence by rearranging the words, and *Qoheleth* has done that in these lines. It seems awkward in English, but *Qoheleth* actually wrote:

> *Not* to the swift is the race,
> *not* to the strong is the battle,
> *not* to the wise does food come,
> *not* to the brilliant does wealth come,
> *not* to the learned comes favor,
> but time and chance happen to them all.

The structure of those lines emphasizes the wisdom of Forrest Gump's mother: you never know what you're going to get unless you learn to expect the unexpected. Don't expect the fastest runner to win the race (remember the fable of the hare and the tortoise?); keep your eye on the underdog. Don't bet all your money on the team with the best record; upsets happen all the time. If the smartest employee always got the promotion or the brightest students always got the top grades, life would be pretty predictable. But that's not how life goes.

Much of our stress in life comes from expecting things to go a certain way and being disappointed—even devastated—when they don't. We expect a raise or promotion, and we don't get it. We expect a clean bill of health, but there are "concerns." We expect smooth sailing, and we run aground instead. We expect a certain reaction, and we get the opposite.

Qoheleth is not saying we need to always expect the worst. He is not recommending a gloomy outlook on life. Quite the contrary, in fact. He is suggesting that we take life as it comes to us, in all of its variety and unpredictability. He goes on:

Moreover, no one knows when their hour will come:

> As fish are caught in a cruel net,
>   or birds are taken in a snare,
> so people are trapped by evil times
>   that fall unexpectedly upon them.[236]

I have lived most of my life in southwest Ohio, an area that experiences all four seasons—and then some. As in many other parts of the world, the weather changes not only from season to season but often from week to week and day to day. Yet I am constantly amazed by people's reaction to such changes. During the months of January and February—every year, mind you—people who've lived here all their lives will moan and whine about the cold, snow, and ice, and express unqualified amazement when the skies clear and the temperature warms. In July and August those same people will complain of the heat and humidity and register astonishment when the weather breaks. It's as if they've never experienced such phenomena before! The only constant in the weather (in this region, at least) is change. The temperature can be in the single digits one week and in the fifties or sixties the next. An ice storm can hit with little warning while the sun is shining just a few miles away.

So it is with life. Some of us expect only sunshine and flowers from life. But as *Qoheleth's* poem in Ecclesiastes 3 showed us, death is just as normal a part of life as birth, and weeping is as natural as laughter. You never know what you're gonna get. Like a box of chocolates, life can be sweet, and it can make you sick.

So don't be surprised by the unexpected. Don't get derailed by it. Learn to expect it.

Learn to Be Content in Obscurity and Adversity

We also inhibit the enjoyment of our own lives by expecting a smooth, unimpeded course of improvement in everything we do and everywhere we go. Each year must be better than the last (according to our measurement). The stock market must go up. Our next job must pay more than the last. Our kids must have it better than we did.

There's nothing wrong with wanting to improve ourselves or our circumstances. New challenges can lead to much blessing. But our expectations can also breed misery. *Qoheleth* says:

> I also saw under the sun this example of wisdom that greatly impressed me: There was once a small city with only a few people in it. And a powerful king came against it, surrounded it and built huge siegeworks against it. Now there lived in that city a man poor but wise, and he saved the city by his wisdom. But nobody remembered that poor man. So I said, "Wisdom is better than strength." But the poor man's wisdom is despised, and his words are no longer heeded.
>
> > The quiet words of the wise are more to be heeded
> > > than the shouts of a ruler of fools.
> > Wisdom is better than weapons of war,
> > > but one sinner destroys much good.[237]

Qoheleth tells the story of a small city that was besieged by a mighty warrior king.

Somehow—*Qoheleth* doesn't specify how—a poor man living in that city saved it by his wisdom. Maybe he found or devised access to food or water that helped the residents withstand the siege. Maybe he proposed a negotiating or diversionary tactic that fooled the enemy. Maybe he decoded a secret message. We don't know.

King Solomon's alter ego tells the story, however, in such a way that it seems to be based on actual events. *Qoheleth* seems to have in mind an actual city, and an actual "poor but wise" man who saved the city and then was forgotten. No parade in his honor. No statue in the town square. No plaque, no marker, not even a picture in the newspaper.

And his point is this: wisdom is better than strength, but even the wisest person should not expect recognition or acclaim. Philosopher Jacques Ellul summarized this section of Ecclesiastes like this:

> Do not expect any reward or renown; do not expect
> others to appreciate you because you are good and just.
> You will simply be wasting your time if you anticipate
> such a result.[238]

Everyone likes to be appreciated. It's always nice to be noticed and congratulated on a job well done. And all of us—some more than others, but all of us to some extent—have a legitimate need to feel the approval, acceptance, or appreciation of our peers and loved ones. But expecting reward or renown is nonetheless a recipe for disappointment. The man or woman who wants to live well in this sick world must learn to be content in obscurity and adversity.

We need the attitude of the Apostle Paul, the great church planter of the first century. Though we look back on his life and accomplishments twenty centuries later and recognize his importance and influence in the early church, he labored and ministered mostly in obscurity and adversity. He was not always recognized or respected, at least not in comparison to other apostles, like Peter, James, and John.[239] His ministry took place far out of the "epicenter" of the church, in Jerusalem. He endured overwhelming adversity[240] yet was still able to say:

> I don't have a sense of needing anything personally. I've learned by now to be quite content whatever my circumstances. I'm just as happy with little as with much, with much as with little. I've found the recipe for being happy whether full or hungry, hands full or hands empty. Whatever I have, wherever I am, I can make it through anything in the One who makes me who I am.[241]

If we hope to live well in this sick and suffering world, we must learn to be content in obscurity and adversity, to be "just as happy" in the shadows as in the spotlight, in good times or bad, whether our hands are full or empty. At such times, when our wisdom and worth are unappreciated (or assailed), we must rely on God's wisdom and strength to make it through.

Learn to Be Faithful in All Things

The next few verses of Ecclesiastes may seem at first glance to be merely a few unrelated proverbs, strung together in no particular order. But on further inspection, they yield extremely helpful insight into living well despite life's unpredictability. *Qoheleth* writes:

> As dead flies give perfume a bad smell,
>> so a little folly outweighs wisdom and honor.
> The heart of the wise inclines to the right,
>> but the heart of the fool to the left.
> Even as fools walk along the road,
>> they lack sense
>> and show everyone how stupid they are:
> If a ruler's anger rises against you,
>> do not leave your post;
>> calmness can lay great offenses to rest.[242]

My wife and I were both ordained many years ago in Kansas City, in a large national convention that commemorated the hundredth anniversary of the Salvation Army's work in the United States. The weekend of our ordination was packed full of one event after another, one program after another, one responsibility after another. In addition, the weather was stiflingly hot, and we and our fellow candidates for ordination were lodged in a camp setting with no air conditioning.

I don't remember much about the schedule, but I recall the Saturday evening program in a large auditorium. We were exhausted, and the program ran late. We just wanted to get to our sweltering lodgings and try to sleep. But we were required to stay to the end. I'm glad we were, because part of the program that night was a play I may never forget.

I don't remember the title. I don't remember any of the dialogue. I have only the vaguest memory of how the stage appeared. But I remember the story. I remember that it moved me.

In the midst of a weekend filled with pageantry and spectacle, the play depicted a husband and wife, Salvation Army pastors, from their earliest days to their retirement. They never received recognition. They never scaled the ladder of command. They never achieved "great" things—at least, not as some would measure greatness. But in one town and church after another, they faithfully served God and his people. They sacrificed. They wept. They showed up.

The final scene of the drama (as I remember it, at least) depicted them on the threshold of retirement and their amazement at the gratitude and appreciation people expressed to them for their quiet, unassuming, faithful service through the years. It brought tears to my eyes. It still does, because people just like that have blessed my life over the years and have made me aspire to be like them: faithful. Faithful.

That's what *Qoheleth*'s couplets in Ecclesiastes 10:1–4 are saying: Be faithful. Each one says it a little differently. Each emphasizes a different form of faithfulness. But each is important for those of us who want to live well in a sick world.

1. Be faithful in the little things of life. "As dead flies give perfume a bad smell," *Qoheleth* says, "so a little folly outweighs wisdom and honor."[243] A more modern parallel to this verse would be, "One bad apple spoils the whole bunch." It takes only a little folly to outweigh a truckload of wisdom and honor. Just one lapse can devastate an otherwise effective relationship, career, or ministry—or life. So it is crucial to be faithful in all things, large and small. It is critical not to let little things become big things.

One of my earliest jobs was ringing bells for the Salvation Army at Christmas time. My father was my immediate supervisor. Now, being a Salvation Army bell ringer is not a highly skilled job, but it is a demanding one. And I remember my father instructing me never to touch the money people dropped into a kettle. Instead, if coins or currency failed to fall completely into the hole in the red cone of the kettle, he showed me how to turn the little handbell upside down and poke the money through the hole, never touching it with my hand, so as not to let any suspicion attach to me or my employer. Such a small thing. Tiny. But "a little folly outweighs wisdom and honor."

After all, Jesus said, "One who is faithful in a very little is also faithful in much, and one who is dishonest in a very little is also dishonest in much."[244] Less than ten years after my father tutored me in the nuances of bell-ringing, I was tasked with managing an annual budget of hundreds of thousands of dollars. It is important to be faithful in the little things of life, for small things can have large and long-lasting results.

2. Be faithful in your thought life. *The Message* paraphrase of Ecclesiastes 10:2 reads: "Wise thinking leads to right living; Stupid thinking leads to wrong living."[245] Anyone who wants to live well will carefully cultivate his or her thought life. James Allen, in his classic volume, *As a Man Thinketh*, wrote:

> A man's mind may be likened to a garden, which may be intelligently cultivated or allowed to run wild; but whether cultivated or neglected, it must, and will, *bring forth*. If no useful seeds are *put* into it, then an abundance of useless weed-seeds will *fall* therein and will continue to produce their kind.
>
> Just as a gardener cultivates his plot, keeping it free from weeds, and growing the flowers and fruits which he requires, so may a man tend the garden of his mind, weeding out all the wrong, useless, and impure thoughts, and cultivating toward perfection the flowers and fruits of right, useful, and pure thoughts. . . . Let a man radically alter his thoughts, and he will be astonished at the rapid transformation it will effect in the material conditions of his life.[246]

This is why the Word of God instructs us:

> Fix your thoughts on what is true, and honorable, and right, and pure, and lovely, and admirable. Think about things that are excellent and worthy of praise.[247]

Take a critical look at the things you think on, the seeds you *put* into the garden of your mind, the things you place in front of your eyes.[248] Is your reading material true, honorable, right, pure, lovely, admirable, excellent, and worthy of praise? Is your television viewing? What about radio and music? Can you cultivate your thought life

better—by listening to quality podcasts, perhaps? By more intentionally planning your reading?[249] By abstaining from certain television
shows? By steering clear of certain discussions at work?

"Wise thinking leads to right living," *Qoheleth* said." Stupid
thinking leads to wrong living."[250] Faithfulness in your thoughts will
bear fruit in your life.

3. Be faithful one step at a time. The third image *Qoheleth* chose
to advise faithfulness in all things was of a person on a footpath:
"Even as fools walk along the road, they lack sense and show everyone how stupid they are."[251] Stupidity, like wisdom, is revealed one
step at a time. And faithfulness must be lived out one step at a time.
There is no other way. Philosopher Friedrich Nietzsche wrote:

> The essential thing "in heaven and in earth" is . . . that
> there should be long OBEDIENCE in the same direction,
> there thereby results, and has always resulted in the long
> run, something which has made life worth living.[252]

Faithfulness must be lived out one day at a time, one decision after
another, step by step. And each faithful stride makes the next surer
and stronger, as Shakespeare's Prince Hamlet explained to his
mother, Queen Gertrude, in pleading with her to stay away from
her husband's—and former brother-in-law's—bed:

> Refrain tonight,
> And that shall lend a kind of easiness
> To the next abstinence; the next more easy;
> For use almost can change the stamp of nature,
> And either [master] the devil, or throw him out
> With wondrous potency.[253]

Fools reveal themselves even as they walk along the road, and
wise men and women show their faithfulness one step at a time. And

every faithful step shall lend a kind of easiness to the next, and "the next more easy." In this way, a faithful and fruitful life is built, even in the midst of a sick and suffering world.

4. Be faithful under fire. A memorable scene occurs in the movie *A League of Their Own*, about a women's professional baseball league that formed and thrived during and following World War II. Dottie Hinson (Geena Davis), the star catcher of the Rockford Peaches, decides to quit the team and return home with her husband. Her manager, Jimmy Dugan (Tom Hanks), tries to dissuade her.

"You'll regret it for the rest of your life," he says. "Baseball is what gets inside you. It's what lights you up. You can't deny that."

"It just got too hard," she replies.

Dugan answers, "It's supposed to be hard! If it wasn't hard, everyone would do it. The hard . . . is what makes it great!"

The same is true of faithfulness. It can be hard. If it wasn't, everyone would enjoy the blessings of a well-lived life. And being faithful can be hardest when you are under fire, as *Qoheleth* points out in Ecclesiastes 10:4: "If a ruler's anger rises against you, do not leave your post; calmness can lay great offenses to rest."[254]

If you aspire to live well in the midst of a sick world, you must learn to be faithful even when under fire. When your boss gets angry. When your kids tax your patience. When the heat is on and the temptation to take a shortcut is nearly irresistible. It is the pressure that turns coal into diamonds. It is the fire that purifies gold. And it is faithfulness in the most challenging circumstances that will bring out the best in you.[255]

Learn from the Example of Others

My wife, the lovely Robin, has been an encouragement and blessing to me in countless ways. One such way is her ability to learn from the example of others. For instance, she has often related how, as she was growing up in Chillicothe, Ohio, she studied the woman who was one of her pastors, having determined at a young age that she wanted to be that kind of woman. Later in life, when she and I were a young married couple training for ministry in the aptly named Suffern, New York, she frequently commented on the parenting styles and skills of our friends, making sure that we took copious mental notes for later use, when we had children of our own. As our own kids were born and grew to maturity, she seized every opportunity to point out to them some of the examples surrounding them, both positive and negative, to guide them in making wise choices and pointing their own lives in wise directions.

That is very likely the sort of thing *Qoheleth* had in mind as he wrote the following verses:

> There is an evil I have seen under the sun,
>   the sort of error that arises from a ruler:
> Fools are put in many high positions,
>   while the rich occupy the low ones.
> I have seen slaves on horseback,
>   while princes go on foot like slaves.
>
> Whoever digs a pit may fall into it;
>   whoever breaks through a wall may be bitten by a snake.
> Whoever quarries stones may be injured by them;
>   whoever splits logs may be endangered by them.
>
> If the ax is dull
>   and its edge unsharpened,
> more strength is needed
>   but skill will bring success.
>
> If a snake bites before it is charmed,
>   the charmer receives no fee.

Words from the mouth of the wise are gracious,
  but fools are consumed by their own lips.
At the beginning their words are folly;
  at the end they are wicked madness—
  and fools multiply words.

No one knows what is coming—
  who can tell someone else what will happen after them?
    The toil of fools wearies them;
    they do not know the way to town.[256]

These verses can be seen as a primer on learning from the example of others. Learn from others' mistakes (v. 5). Learn from the inequities you observe in life (vv. 6–7). Learn from the careless actions of others (vv. 8–9). Learn from watching others work (vv. 10–11). Learn by listening (vv. 12–14a). Learn by observation—even by observing fools (v. 15).

When our children were growing up, the popular television sitcom *Friends* was at the height of its popularity. Many of our kids' young friends were watching it and talking about Ross, Rachel, Monica, Chandler, Phoebe, and Joey at school. But our daughter and son were not allowed to watch it. One day my wife and I somehow caught wind of an episode in which Ross (David Shwimmer) and Rachel (Jennifer Aniston) agreed to take a "break" in their relationship. In the emotion of the moment, Ross went to a club, drank until he was tipsy, and then went to bed with a young woman he barely knew. Predictably enough, when Rachel found out (an episode later, I think), she was devastated. Their relationship was shattered. And the fallout from that single act of unfaithfulness affected the entire group of friends.

It may seem strange, but the lovely Robin and I taped the show and invited our teen children to watch their first episodes of *Friends*.

Why? Because those episodes provided an effective and memorable depiction of the cost of unfaithfulness and a prime opportunity to discuss with our kids the loving wisdom of God's standards for love, marriage, and sexual intimacy.

Forrest Gump's mom was right. Life *is* like a box of chocolates in that you never know what you're going to get. It is changeful. Unpredictable. Often surprising, even shocking. But there are ways to deal with life's unpredictability. It is possible to live well in this sick world by learning to expect the unexpected, by learning to be content even in obscurity and adversity, by learning to be faithful in all things, and by learning from the example of others. The man or woman who does those things may also learn another way life is like a box of chocolates: sometimes the surprising parts are sweeter than the rest.

———— ∾ ————

*A*bba, Father, I confess that I want life to be smooth, predictable, comfy, and cozy, and I am often stressed, disappointed, even devastated, when things don't go as planned. So help me to learn to expect the unexpected and not to get derailed by it.

Teach me also to be content in obscurity and adversity. Cultivate in me a sense of not needing anything personally, but of being "quite content whatever my circumstances . . . [being] just as happy with little as with much, with much as with little . . . [of being] happy whether full or hungry, hands full or hands empty." Remind me often that, whatever I have, wherever I am, "I can make it through anything in the One who makes me who I am."[257]

Teach me faithfulness, too—in the little things, in my thought life, one step at a time, even under fire. And help me to learn from the example of others—from their mistakes, from the inequities I observe, from the careless actions of others, from watching people work, by listening, by observation—even by observing fools. Make every place a school-room to me and every circumstance a lesson. In Jesus' name, amen.

chapter TEN

LIVING WELL IS THE BEST REVENGE

My wife and I like to believe that we were pretty good parents. Our kids—now grown—even tell us so (when they're not laughing at us or telling us how to manage some childcare innovation). Sometimes they even pay us the high compliment of asking for our advice as they raise their own children.

Still, we stumbled as parents at least as often as we soared. We are living proof of the axiom that it takes a lifetime to get good at parenting, and by that time, your job is done.

One of the ways in which I wish we had done better was in being the kind of parents our son—the younger of our two children—needed. Our children were both well into their teens when we were helped to realize that our daughter, Aubrey, responded well to our style of parenting because her personality and emotional needs more or less corresponded to ours; we understood each other and most of the time got along just fine. However, our son, Aaron, had his own personality and emotional needs (I know, I know, it sounds elementary at this point). Our parenting styles quite naturally supported our daughter's needs for affection and encouragement but not so much our son's need for respect and approval.

I also wish we had learned much earlier how different our children's learning styles were. They were (and are) both extremely bright people and good students, but they go about learning things in thoroughly different ways. From the time she was very young, I could sit Aubrey down and explain something to her, and she would listen intently, ask any questions that occurred to her, and the lesson was learned. Not Aaron. I could tell him something, explain it thoroughly, even diagram it for him, and he would nod and assure me, "Got it." But he only truly "got it" when he did it. His tactile and spatial learning abilities were off the chart.

You'd think it would have dawned on me sooner than it did. After all, he had barely learned to tie his own shoes when I started asking him to untangle knots in my shoestrings. If something had to be assembled, Aaron could do it in a fraction of the time it would take me. But it wasn't just that his mechanical and visual skills were exceptional; it seemed that, while there was virtually nothing he couldn't grasp and learn quickly and fully, he never learned anything except by experience—an attribute that makes him a brilliant musician, technician, and computer analyst.

I think King Solomon was like that. He could have learned so much from his father's example and writings. But there seems to be virtually no indication that he did.

He would certainly have heard the story of David's tawdry episode with Bathsheba, Solomon's mother (though it may have been kept from him throughout his early years, he would have learned the truth sooner or later, palaces and families being what they are). Surely Solomon could have been warned by the deadly consequences of his father's apparent neglect of his sons Absalom and Adonijah. Surely

King David would have tried to teach Solomon about the emptiness of lust, the dangers of wine, the folly of pleasure-seeking.

Right?

Yet *Qoheleth* wrote, as Solomon's alter ego:

> I denied myself nothing my eyes desired;
>   I refused my heart no pleasure.[258]

Whatever David—not to mention his tutors and professors—tried to teach Solomon, he apparently had to strategically and systematically try everything himself. Shoot, he had access to the Law of Moses and the psalms of his father David just as we do, and yet only in the laboratory of life did he come to the conclusions that are recorded for us in the book of Ecclesiastes.

But in that respect, Solomon is not so different from you or me. He is much like modern Christians and church-goers, who might nod in agreement when the reader or preacher intones, "Everything under the sun is meaningless, like chasing the wind."[259] But then, like Solomon, we lose ourselves in work, as if success would satisfy our cravings. Or we fret over our finances and install an even bigger HDTV, as though money and pleasure would truly meet our needs. We pursue all the things Solomon pursued, while telling ourselves that *Qoheleth* was right to describe them as meaningless. We insist on proving for ourselves what *Qoheleth* concluded so many years ago, and wrote down for our instruction.

Strike While the Irony Is Hot

Some readers and commentators consider Ecclesiastes a cynical book. That may be true, but I think its more prominent characteristic is irony. It warns against the writing of books. Its wisdom consists of showing wisdom to be meaningless. And it is the record of a man who learned—only by firsthand experience—great truths he hoped to pass on via secondhand instruction.

Still, there are some people, like my daughter, who learn easily from the wisdom and example of others. If you've made it this far without chucking this book into the garbage bin, you're probably one of those people. You're probably the very sort of person *Qoheleth* had in mind. And, though at times he may have tried to perform his soul surgery with a blunt edge, this "seeker after truth" takes up a very important question—and just in time—in the latter part of Ecclesiastes 10: *What now?* In view of all he has said, all he has experienced, all he has discovered and related to us, what are we supposed to do? How are we supposed to live?

Do we curl up in a fetal position and wait for our meaningless lives to end? Do we throw caution to the wind and live only for the pleasure of the moment? Do we check ourselves into a monastery or convent? If everything under the sun is meaningless, as *Qoheleth* says, how then should we live?

Live Responsibly

After nine and a half chapters of stark realism, of uncompromising honesty, of saying things like,

> All things are wearisome,
> > more than one can say,[260]

and,

> We all come to the end of our lives
> > as naked and empty-handed as on the day we were born,[261]

and,

> Like a fish caught in a net,
> > or a bird caught in a trap,
> people are trapped by evil
> > when it suddenly falls on them,[262]

Qoheleth comes around to suggesting at least a few helpful answers to the question, "How then should we live?" He begins:

> Woe to the land whose king was a servant
>> and whose princes feast in the morning.
> Blessed is the land whose king is of noble birth
>> and whose princes eat at a proper time—
>> for strength and not for drunkenness.[263]

When he mentions kings and princes who "feast in the morning," he's talking about government officials who are irresponsible, self-indulgent, and self-serving. In the Hebrew culture of that day, rulers and judges held court in the morning; late afternoon and evening were the times for feasting. When the so-called responsible people reverse the proper order of things—or mix ruling with reveling— things are not as they should be. If you're being ruled by a weak king, corrupt princes, or officials who neglect their responsibility, you're in a heap o' hurt!

But everybody wins, *Qoheleth* says, when rulers and officials are responsible. Whether you're a king or president, an employer or employee, a pastor or a teacher, his message is this: live responsibly. First things first. Take care of business.

He goes on to say, in verse 18,

> Through laziness, the rafters sag;
>> because of idle hands, the house leaks.[264]

This is the same message, only now brought down from the national to the personal level. How shall we live? Take care of business. Maintain your property. Pay your homeowners' association fees. Mow your lawn. Pick up after yourself. Do not litter. Live responsibly.

The next proverb continues the same thought:

> A feast is made for laughter,

> wine makes life merry,
> and money is the answer for everything.[265]

That is, go ahead, eat and drink with gladness, as he said in Ecclesiastes 9:7, but you've still gotta be responsible, you've still gotta make a living, you've still gotta pay the bills, because if the money stops coming in, so does the food and wine.

When he says, "money is the answer for everything," he is not contradicting his conclusion that the pursuit of wealth is meaningless. The statement is connected to feasting and drinking and perhaps also to rafters that don't sag and roofs that don't leak. In other words, as the philosopher Ringo Starr sang, "It don't come easy." Or, in the words of the Apostle Paul, "The one who is unwilling to work shall not eat."[266]

But living responsibly is not only a matter of mowing the lawn and paying the bills. He closes this section with verse 20:

> Do not revile the king even in your thoughts,
>   or curse the rich in your bedroom,
> because a bird in the sky may carry your words,
>   and a bird on the wing may report what you say."[267]

This is the likely origin of the saying, "A little bird told me." It is also an admonition to be responsible in what we say, and it is a key part of the well-lived life: *don't say things you'll be sorry for later.*

Even if no one's listening, even in your thoughts, even in your own bedroom, *don't say things you'll be sorry for later.*

I've seen so many relationships ruined by careless words. Words spoken thoughtlessly. Things said in anger. Offhand comments that were supposed to be "in confidence." People have lost jobs over such things. Families have been fractured. Churches have split. All because of someone who couldn't keep his or her mouth shut.

Live responsibly, *Qoheleth* says. In your civic life, in your home life, in leisure, and in language: live responsibly.

Live Generously

Living responsibly will take you far. It may not always be easy, but it will pay rich dividends—and compounding interest—in your life. Ironically, however, *Qoheleth*'s next lines prescribe a little healthy irresponsibility for the person who would live well:

> Cast your bread upon the waters,
>> for after many days you will find it again.
> Give portions to seven, yes to eight,
>> for you do not know what disaster may come upon
>>> the land.[268]

The idea expressed there is one of openhanded generosity. Give freely, liberally, generously to the needs of others.

The phrase, "Cast your bread upon the waters," was probably an Arabic proverb for what looked like wasteful expenditure. No one would take good bread and throw it in the river or onto the ocean waves; that would be wasteful, right? It's similar to our familiar proverbs about "throwing your money down a rat hole" or "throwing good money after bad."

But here we are enjoined to do that very thing. Now, that doesn't mean we're supposed to spend like drunken sailors; it means go ahead and be generous, maybe even uncomfortably generous, when you see a need, because in the wisdom and purpose of God it will return to you some day, somehow, when you are in need.

We should also give as widely as possible, *Qoheleth* says:

> Give portions to seven, yes to eight.[269]

In other words, "Give to as many as you can, and then some." Spread it around. Live generously.

Seven was a symbolic number in Hebrew culture. It signified perfection. Completion. So when *Qoheleth* says, "Give portions to seven, yes to eight," he may be suggesting a spirit of generosity that even goes past perfection, beyond what any reasonable person would consider to be ample.

Why would a person do that? *Qoheleth* seems to anticipate the question. He goes on to mention four reasons for this kind of generosity:

> If clouds are full of water,
>   they pour rain upon the earth.
> Whether a tree falls to the south or to the north,
>   in the place where it falls, there will it lie.[270]

The first reason we are to give generously is because *it is the natural outflow of a full life*, like clouds that fill up and empty themselves, again and again, over and over. God fills up the clouds, not so they can get bigger and bigger, but so they can empty themselves over and over. And he gives good things to you for the same reason. The Bible says,

> God is able to make all grace abound to you, so that
> in all things at all times, having all that you need, you
> will abound in every good work. . . . You will be made
> rich in every way so that you can be generous on every
> occasion.[271]

If God has blessed you, he did it so you could be a blessing to others. He fills your life so it will overflow in generosity. He fills you so you can empty yourself, like the clouds of heaven.

The mention of the tree falling to the south or north is his way of saying, "wherever God has put you, meet needs around you; be alert to the reasons God may have for placing you there." In other words, *live generously because in doing so you will more likely fulfill God's reasons for putting you where you are.*

There is another reason for living generously given in verse 4:

> Whoever watches the wind will not plant;
> whoever looks at the clouds will not reap.[272]

That is, don't wait for the perfect time to give. Don't think you have to have so much in the bank before you start giving. Because no stage of life is ideally suited for being generous. Or, perhaps more accurately, *every stage of life is ideally suited for being generous.*

For example, you may think you should wait until you graduate from college to start worshiping God with your giving, to start tithing, to start giving to missions and worthwhile causes, to start helping others less fortunate, to become a person of abounding generosity. But that's not a biblical perspective. And after you graduate, it's "wait till I get a good job," and then it's "wait till after the wedding," and then it's "I can't afford it with this mortgage payment," and then it's "once we can stop buying diapers," and then it's "the kids' braces are gonna cost how much?" and then it's "you know how much college tuition is these days?" And on and on it goes.

> Whoever watches the wind will not plant;
> whoever looks at the clouds will not reap.[273]

Live generously, because *now* is always the time to be generous. And also for another reason:

> As you do not know the path of the wind,
> or how the body is formed in a mother's womb,
> so you cannot understand the work of God,
> the Maker of all things.

> Sow your seed in the morning,
> and at evening let your hands not be idle,

> for you do not know which will succeed,
>> whether this or that,
>> or whether both will do equally well.[274]

Notice that phrase, "you do not know." *Qoheleth* used it earlier, in Ecclesiastes 11:2 ("you do not know what disaster may come upon the land"[275]), and he uses it twice in these lines. He's saying, "live generously, because just as you don't know where the wind comes from or how a baby's body takes shape in a mother's womb, you also don't know what God will do with your generous gifts or what he will do for you someday as a result of them!"

In 2013, actor and producer Tyler Perry posted this on his Facebook page:

> It's funny how a song, a taste, a scent, or something as simple as a change in weather can trigger a memory. Certain times of year make me think about when I was homeless. Especially the winter. I started thinking about this one lady in particular who helped me out during that time. She was a good soul who saw me in need and gave me money and food. She didn't have much, but what she had she shared out of the kindness of her heart. I told her that when I got successful I would pay her back. She smiled and said, "You don't have to pay me anything. I just felt led to help you."

> I couldn't stop thinking about her the other day, so I did some research and found her. Imagine her shock when I called her. She didn't even think that I remembered her. It's funny how something that was a small gesture to her was a huge blessing to me. As we went on talking, she reluctantly told me that she had just lost her

job and was facing foreclosure. Of course, I did some things to help her out.

Why am I telling you this? I'm glad you asked. She gave to me out of the kindness of her heart. She gave to me from a pure place and expected nothing in return. The thing that brought tears to my eyes and blessed me so about this situation was this: this woman planted a seed in my life almost twenty years ago. But what she didn't know at the time was that the seed she planted would one day come back and bless her life just when she needed it most.

So what am I saying? I'm saying that if you are a giver of whatever you have . . . time, money, love, help, whatever it is . . . if you plant it in pureness it has got to come back to you. It may take a while, but you will reap a harvest from that seed. Don't be weary in well-doing. It will come back to you. I know sometimes it may seem that all the good you do goes unnoticed by people, but if they don't notice, it doesn't matter. If they don't acknowledge your kindness, it does not matter. You know why? Because I promise you God sees it all, and He is the only one that matters. And He is bound by His word, and that word says you will reap what you sow. So sow on, sow good seeds. They will grow and come back to you when you least expect it.[276]

You don't know whether the dollar you put in the Salvation Army red kettle may spur the guy walking behind you to write a $100 check!

You don't know whether the tithe you scrape together in a time of need may come back to you at the most opportune time.

You don't know whether your kindness to a friend may make possible an even larger kindness.

You don't know the power of God or the timing of God. He changes and blesses lives, and he changes the *history of the world* by the phenomenon of Christian giving.

So live responsibly, says *Qoheleth*. Live generously. And live thoughtfully.

Live Thoughtfully

If living responsibly and living generously are essentials for living well in a sick world—and they are—living thoughtfully is just as critical. Look at verse 7:

> Light is sweet,
>   and it pleases the eyes to see the sun.
> However many years anyone may live,
>   let them enjoy them all.
> But let them remember the days of darkness,
>   for there will be many.
>   Everything to come is meaningless.[277]

Light and sun are symbols of life lived in the love of God. Just as we love to step outside when we see the sun break through on a cloudy, gloomy day, so we can enjoy the love of God, the sense of his acceptance, the joy of his presence, the knowledge that we are approved and accepted by him, the gift of righteousness by faith. This makes life worth living.

But verse 8 also contains a warning, and it's one I think we can understand in two important ways. When *Qoheleth* says, "However many years anyone may live, let them enjoy them all. But let them remember the days of darkness, for there will be many,"[278] I don't think he's being maudlin or pessimistic. I think he's saying, "Make the most of good days, because everybody has bad days."

That's not pessimism, that's realism. It's common sense. "Enjoy it while you got it." "Make hay while the sun shines." "If you like it then you shoulda put a ring on it." I'm not sure that last one applies, but the general idea is not to let yesterday's rain—or tomorrow's fore-cast—ruin today's parade.

But *Qoheleth* is not only saying, "make the most of good days, because everybody has bad days," he is also talking about preparing for the end of our earthly lives. He says, in verses 9 and 10:

> You who are young, be happy while you are young,
>> and let your heart give you joy in the days of your youth.
> Follow the ways of your heart
>> and whatever your eyes see,
> but know that for all these things
>> God will bring you to judgment.
> So then, banish anxiety from your heart
>> and cast off the troubles of your body,
>> for youth and vigor are meaningless.[279]

When you're young, use your limitless energy, enjoy your good looks, follow your dreams, seize opportunities, take advantage of being young.

But—there's always a "but," isn't there? Remember that though there are great, open doors of opportunity set before you (which you will not have later in life), approach those doors thoughtfully, carefully, with the realization that many people spend a lifetime recovering from bad choices, and some even spend an eternity suffering for them.

But not you . . . I pray, not you. No matter what your past has been, no matter what your future might be, you can live responsibly, generously, and thoughtfully, in the awareness that this life is not "IT," this life is not all there is, all that is done "under the sun" is not all that is done. You can live well in this sick world—and best prepare for the next—by letting the responsible, generous, and thoughtful life of Brooke Bronkowski challenge and inspire you.

Let Your Heart Give You Joy

Francis Chan, in his book *Crazy Love*, shares a little of Brooke's story. She started a Bible study when she was in junior high school and soon was spending her babysitting money to buy Bibles to give away to friends and classmates. Chan, who at the time was pastor at Cornerstone Church in Simi Valley, California, wrote:

> During her freshman year in high school, Brooke was in a car accident while driving to the movies. Her life on earth ended when she was just fourteen, but her impact didn't. Nearly fifteen hundred people attended Brooke's memorial service. People from her public high school read poems she had written about her love for God. Everyone spoke of her example and her joy.
>
> I shared the gospel and invited those who wanted to know Jesus to come up and give their lives to Him. There must have been at least two hundred students on their knees at the front of the church praying for salvation. Ushers gave a Bible to each one of them. They were Bibles that Brooke had kept in her garage, hoping to give out to all of her unsaved friends. In one day, Brooke led more people to the Lord than most ever will.[280]

I don't know if Brooke Bronkowski ever studied—or even read—Ecclesiastes. Maybe, maybe not. But she couldn't have better captured *Qoheleth*'s wisdom than in the following essay she wrote around the age of twelve:

> "Since I Have My Life Before Me"
>   By Brooke Bronkowski
>
> I'll live my life to the fullest. I'll be happy. I'll brighten up.
> I will be more joyful than I have ever been. I will be kind

to others. I will loosen up. I will tell others about Christ. I will go on adventures and change the world. I will be bold and not change who I really am. I will have no troubles but instead help others with their troubles.

You see, I'll be one of those people who live to be history makers at a young age. Oh, I'll have moments, good and bad, but I'll wipe away the bad and only remember the good. In fact that's all I remember, just good moments, nothing in between, just living my life to the fullest. I'll be one of those people who go somewhere with a mission, an awesome plan, a world-changing plan, and nothing will hold me back. I'll set an example for others. I will pray for direction.

I have my life before me. I will give others the joy I have, and God will give me more joy. I will do everything God tells me to do. I will follow the footsteps of God. I will do my best!!![281]

———— ∿ ————

This is more like it, Lord! Thank you for the encouragement and challenge of this chapter and its reminder that, no matter what my past has been, no matter what awaits me in the future, I can live responsibly, generously, and thoughtfully, in the awareness that this life is not "IT," this life is not all there is, all that is done "under the sun" is not all that is done.

Help me, God, to live well in this sick world—and prepare for the next—by living fully, boldly, courageously, and joyfully. Make me "a history maker." Let me set an example for others. Let me give joy to others, that you may give me more to give away again. Let me do everything you tell me to do. Let me follow the tracings of your steps. Let me do my best. In Jesus' name, amen.

GROWING OLD IS MANDATORY; GROWING UP IS OPTIONAL

I had a friend a few years ago (I've had one or two since then, too). We had been friends a long time. For years, we met weekly for lunch. We laughed and cried together. We teased each other. We traveled together, supported each other, and held each other accountable. We disagreed at times but always found a way to forgive and move on.

But one day I received a note from my friend. He said that he was suspending our relationship, and I was not to contact him for at least six months. He didn't explain. He didn't say if or how I had offended him. He simply cut off the relationship, cold.

In retrospect, I shouldn't have honored his wishes as I did. I should have contacted him in spite of his note and at least tried to repent of whatever I did that caused (or contributed to) the break in our relationship. But I didn't. I refrained from contacting him, not only for six months, but for however long he wished.

It has been a few years now, and we still haven't talked. Oh, we run into each other now and then, but we've never talked about what caused the break. He's never told me how I hurt him, and I've never asked him. It's old news, right? Water under the bridge. Spilled milk. But it still hurts.

Maybe you've experienced something similar. A friendship ends. Someone stops talking to you. Someone starts talking *about* you. And you never find out why. You are left wondering, guessing, hurting.

Anytime we suffer a significant loss—the end of a relationship, the loss of a job, a death, etc.—our hearts long for closure, a sense of completion, a farewell. Dr. Abigail Brenner, a psychiatrist and author, says, "Closure means finality; a letting go of what once was. Finding closure implies a complete acceptance of what has happened and an honoring of the transition away from what's finished to something new."[282]

Some Endings Are Better Than Others

I think *Qoheleth*, the author of Ecclesiastes and King Solomon's alter ego, understood that. After writing nearly five thousand words about his personal, experimental, and experiential search for meaning in a sick world, *Qoheleth* wrote one more chapter. After eleven chapters, in which he pronounced wealth, pleasure, status, education, work, and more as utterly unsatisfying to the human soul, he might have ended his treatise after urging his reader to live responsibly, generously, and thoughtfully in what we know as chapter 11 (the chapter and verse divisions were added long after Ecclesiastes was written). He could have tied things up with the last words of chapter 11:

> You who are young, be happy while you are young,
>   and let your heart give you joy in the days of your youth.
> Follow the ways of your heart
>   and whatever your eyes see,

but know that for all these things
    God will bring you to judgment.
So then, banish anxiety from your heart
    and cast off the troubles of your body,
        for youth and vigor are meaningless.[283]

But *Qoheleth* didn't end there. And it is a good thing, because anyone who wants to live well in a sick world can profit tremendously from his closing words, found in Ecclesiastes 12. They are words that offer closure to a soul like mine that has sought meaning and fulfillment in work, money, pleasure, and the other things *Qoheleth* pronounces meaningless. They are words that can actually provide a rule of life to anyone who truly wants to live a meaningful and fulfilling life, whatever his or her circumstances. And they are words that bring a sense of "complete acceptance of what has happened and an honoring of the transition away from what's finished to something new,"[284] words that turn the reader's heart away from the disappointment and emptiness of the past to the few things that matter in light of the brevity, uncertainty, and vacuity of life "under the sun." *Qoheleth*'s final chapter supplies three practical, helpful, and artful tips that will help anyone live well in a sick world.

Remember Who Made You

Through eleven chapters, *Qoheleth* has ruthlessly and systematically shown the emptiness of a life that is lived "under the sun." He has shown the uselessness of trying to find meaning in wealth, pleasure, status, learning, and accomplishment. He has even demonstrated the pursuit of happiness itself to be meaningless. Philosopher Jacques Ellul writes:

> The most obvious goal, the first thing we tend to aim for,
> is happiness. But we also need to remember that today, as

formerly, happiness is vanity, folly, insignificance ("What does it matter?"), and a striving after wind. We have a long way to go to understand this lesson! Our world goes on as if it had not heard, as if only happiness and the "right to happiness" actually constituted our goal, our self-realization, and the revelation of the depths of our being.[285]

But *Qoheleth* knows better, and so he guides us in his final chapter to the things that *do* constitute our goal, our self-realization, and the revelation of the depths of our being. He begins, in Ecclesiastes 12:

> Remember your Creator
> in the days of your youth. . . .[286]

"Remember your Creator," *Qoheleth* says. Remember the One who made you. That word, "remember," means much more than giving God a passing thought. Charles Swindoll writes:

> "Remember your Creator when you are young" means to act decisively on behalf of the living God. This means that we realize He is the one essential ingredient we need for a truly happy lifestyle. It means that we listen to what He says and act accordingly. It means we will not follow the dictates of our own heart, but that we will follow the dictates of His truth.[287]

So far in his treatise on life and meaning, *Qoheleth* has mentioned God roughly forty times, and each time he has referred to him as "Elohim," the common Hebrew word for God. Only in Ecclesiastes 12:1 does he depart from that pattern, using the word, "Creator." Why this new term at this point in the book? Commentator Adam Clarke suggests that it is quite purposeful, in order to communicate:

> You are not your own, you have no right to yourselves.
> God made you; he is your Creator; he made you that you

might be happy; but you can be happy only in him. And
as he created you, so he preserves you; he feeds, clothes,
upholds you. He has made you capable of knowing, loving,
and serving him in this world, and of enjoying him in his
own glory forever. And when you had undone yourselves
by sin, he sent his Son to redeem you by his blood; and he
sends his Spirit to enlighten, convince, and draw you away
from childishness, from vain and trifling, as well as from
sinful, pursuits.[288]

Qoheleth is "rounding third and heading for home," so to speak. He
is wrapping up his treatise on life and meaning by turning the reader's mind and heart away from vain, trifling, and sinful pursuits and
toward a decisive action—submission to God. And, while *Qoheleth*
is writing these words from the perspective of an aged king, he urges
action "in the days of your youth," not only while there is still time
but also while there is still health and energy to be spent in worthwhile pursuits. Because, he goes on to show in poetic detail, age will
sooner or later take its toll:

> Remember your Creator
>   in the days of your youth,
> before the days of trouble come
>   and the years approach when you will say,
>   "I find no pleasure in them"—
> before the sun and the light
>   and the moon and the stars grow dark,
>   and the clouds return after the rain;
> when the keepers of the house tremble,
>   and the strong men stoop,
> when the grinders cease because they are few,
>   and those looking through the windows grow dim;

> when the doors to the street are closed
>> and the sound of grinding fades;
> when people rise up at the sound of birds,
>> but all their songs grow faint;
> when people are afraid of heights
>> and of dangers in the streets;
> when the almond tree blossoms
>> and the grasshopper drags itself along
>> and desire no longer is stirred.
> Then people go to their eternal home
>> and mourners go about the streets.[289]

Many scholars and commentators recognize in these verses an allegory of old age, as Warren W. Wiersbe makes plain:

> Verses 3–7 give us one of the most imaginative descriptions of old age and death found anywhere in literature. Students don't agree on all the details of interpretation, but most of them do see here a picture of a house that is falling apart and finally turns to dust. A dwelling place is one biblical metaphor for the human body (Job 4:19, 2 Cor. 5:1–2 [a tent], 2 Peter 1:13 [a tent]), and taking down a house or tent is a picture of death. The meaning may be as follows:
>
> *keepers of the house*—Your arms and hands tremble.
> *strong men*—Your legs, knees, and shoulders weaken, and you walk bent over.
> *grinders*—You start to lose your teeth.
> *windows*—Your vision begins to deteriorate.
> *doors*—Either your hearing starts to fail or you close your mouth because you've lost your teeth.

grinding—You can't chew your food, or your ears can't pick up the sounds outdoors.

rise up—You wake up with the birds early each morning, and wish you could sleep longer.

music—Your voice starts to quaver and weaken.

afraid—You are terrified of heights and afraid of falling while you walk down the street.

almond tree—If you have any hair left, it turns white, like almond blossoms.

grasshopper—You just drag yourself along, like a grasshopper at the close of the summer season.

desire—You lose your appetite, or perhaps your sexual desire.

long home—You go to your eternal [long] home and people mourn your death.[290]

It is best, *Qoheleth* says, to remember who made you, before the ravages of old age overtake you. Recognize him as the one essential ingredient for a truly satisfying life. Listen to him. Respond to him. Submit to him. Follow him. Give him your energy and vitality, while you still have those things to give.

Remember Who Holds You

A popular phrase has arisen in recent years: "bucket list." It refers to a list of things a person wants to accomplish or experience before dying and inspired *The Bucket List*, a 2007 movie starring Morgan Freeman and Jack Nicholson, in which two terminally ill patients set out to complete their list before death catches up to them.

The term "bucket list" comes from another English idiom: "to kick the bucket," a euphemism for dying. But no one seems to know where the term "kick the bucket" came from. Some say it refers to death by hanging, in which a person wanting to commit suicide would loop a noose over a tree branch, step onto an overturned bucket, and slip the noose around his neck; death would come, of course, when the person kicked the bucket away. Another theory is that the term comes from the administration of last rites in the Roman Catholic tradition, when a bucket of holy water would be placed at the feet of a dying person, and visitors who came to pray for the sick person would use it to sprinkle the body; often enough, we may assume, the dying person's death throes would result in his or her feet "kicking the bucket."

Something like that is happening in Ecclesiastes 12:6–8. Having artfully depicted the ravages of old age, *Qoheleth* goes on to employ several euphemisms for death—the exact sources for which have become obscure. His point, however, is as clear as ever, as he continues his reference to remembering God:

> Remember him—before the silver cord is severed,
>   or the golden bowl is broken;
> before the pitcher is shattered at the spring,
>   and the wheel broken at the well,
> and the dust returns to the ground it came from,
>   and the spirit returns to God who gave it.[291]

Each of *Qoheleth*'s metaphors depicts the value and fragility of life and the prospect of it ending suddenly and, of course, irreversibly. No one knows for sure where his reference to the golden bowl and silver cord come from; they are like the origins of the term "kick the bucket." They may be an allusion to furnishings in the Jerusalem Temple, like the "solid gold lampstand with a bowl at the top"[292] described in Zechariah's prophecy. Or they may refer to gold-plated household lamps hung from ceilings by cords of silk and silver woven together. But rabbis and scholars generally agree that the golden bowl symbolizes the human skull (or the lining of the skull) and the silver cord either the medulla oblongata or spinal marrow in the human body.

The pitcher at the spring and the wheel at the well are obvious references to the way people drew water in *Qoheleth*'s day (and in many parts of the world today). A clay pitcher or vessel would be taken to a well, and water would be drawn up in a bucket (or by using the pitcher itself) from an underground spring by means of a rope winding around a wheel. The pitcher and wheel were probably meant to symbolize the human heart and circulatory system. In any case, it is another picture of the moment when "the dust returns to the ground it came from, and the spirit returns to God who gave it,"[293] which prompts a final bitter cry from *Qoheleth*:

> "Meaningless! Meaningless!" says the Teacher.
>   "Everything is meaningless!"[294]

Those words—an echo of Ecclesiastes 1:2—bracket *Qoheleth*'s entire search. It is the coda to the overture with which he began his treatise on life and meaning:

> "Meaningless! Meaningless!"
>   says the Teacher.
> "Utterly meaningless!
>   Everything is meaningless."[295]

He has uncompromisingly laid out before the reader a stark view of life "under the sun." He warned us at the beginning, and he reiterates at the end: It is meaningless. Empty. Futile. We should not—cannot—hope to find meaning in this life alone—not in wealth, pleasure, work, or any other aspect of a life that is lived solely "under the sun." Though *Qoheleth* had a mere suspicion of life beyond the grave,[296] he concludes that ultimate meaning is in the hands of the

Creator. There is no meaning apart from God. He made you, and he holds you. He alone determined when your life would begin; he alone determines when it will end. And he alone will impart whatever reward awaits you.

Remember Who Rewards You

With *Qoheleth*'s pronunciation of "Everything is meaningless!" in Ecclesiastes 12:8, his treatise is complete. The final verses (Ecclesiastes 12:9–14) take a surprising turn. They speak of "the Teacher," *Qoheleth*, in second person:

> Not only was the Teacher wise, but he also imparted knowledge to the people. He pondered and searched out and set in order many proverbs. The Teacher searched to find just the right words, and what he wrote was upright and true.
>
> The words of the wise are like goads, their collected sayings like firmly embedded nails—given by one shepherd. Be warned, my son, of anything in addition to them.
>
> Of making many books there is no end, and much study wearies the body.[297]

We don't know if these final verses of Ecclesiastes were written by *Qoheleth* or not (if they were, they form a sort of "author's note," in which Solomon's alter ego steps out of his "Teacher" persona to say a few final words). On the other hand, these final verses may have been added by one of *Qoheleth*'s students or a later editor.

In any case, they form a fitting finale to the message of this unusual book. *Qoheleth* summarizes his efforts in three ways, which ought to be characteristic of every seeker after truth and preacher of the Word.

1. He did his best. *Qoheleth* says he was not only wise—a static quality—but he also labored to impart knowledge to the people—an active pursuit. He says he "pondered and searched out and set in order many proverbs."[298] The English Standard Version renders that phrase, "weighing and studying and arranging many proverbs with great care."[299] The original Hebrew conveys the image of "sifting" words and ideas. He wrestled with his work. He "searched to find just the right words."[300] He struggled and strove to make sure what he wrote was upright and true.

2. He pursued a purpose. *Qoheleth* searched as he did and wrote what he did in order to "impart knowledge." He intended for his words—like all the words of the wise—to be like a goad. A goad was a spiked stick—still in use today by cattle drivers—to prod animals into action and guide them in a certain direction. So *Qoheleth* wanted his words to spur action and steer his readers in a certain direction (a direction that is indicated by his mention of "one shepherd," by which he means God, the Creator whom we are to remember and acknowledge as the one essential ingredient for a satisfying life). He also likens wise words to "firmly embedded nails" [301]—or, as the New American Standard Bible has it, "well-driven nails"—again indicating that he intended his words to make a point, to be hammered home, and to stick.

3. He gave it all he had. He said in verse 12, "Of making many books there is no end, and much study wearies the body."[302] This statement is true enough, generally speaking. But *Qoheleth* probably meant it to be taken quite personally and specifically. He wrote from the perspective of an old king, Solomon, who "composed some 3,000 proverbs and wrote 1,005 songs,"[303] wrote the Bible's epic love poem, *Song of Solomon*, and compiled the Bible's book of Proverbs. So in wrapping up what may have been his final literary work, the culmination of his studies, he had every reason to conclude that writing books was an endless task and much study wears a person out. But he had given it his all. He had fought the good fight and finished the race, so to speak.[304]

Having said all that and set out a worthy goal for any teacher, writer, or speaker, *Qoheleth's* treatise on life and meaning concludes:

> Now all has been heard;
>   here is the conclusion of the matter:
> Fear God and keep his commandments,
>   for this is the duty of all humanity.
> For God will bring every deed into judgment,
>   including every hidden thing,
>   whether it is good or evil.[305]

After urging us to remember the One who made us and to remember the One who holds us, Ecclesiastes 12:13–14 tells us to remember the One who rewards us. "Fear God," it says, "and keep his commandments." Take him seriously. Pay attention to him. Listen to him. Regard him. Respect him. Revere him. Orient your life around him. "Act decisively on [his] behalf . . . realize He is the one essential ingredient we need for a truly happy lifestyle . . . listen to what He says and act accordingly . . . follow the dictates of His truth."[306]

Moses told the newborn nation of Israel:

> And now, O Israel, what does the LORD your God ask of
> you but to fear the LORD your God, to walk in all his ways,
> to love him, to serve the LORD your God with all your
> heart and with all your soul, and to observe the LORD's
> commands and decrees that I am giving you today for
> your own good?[307]

After Moses died, his successor Joshua made a point of saying,

Now fear the Lord and serve him with all faithfulness.[308]

Generations later, the prophet Samuel told God's people,

> Be sure to fear the Lord and serve him faithfully with
> all your heart; consider what great things he has done for
> you.[309]

Is that all there is? Is that the best *Qoheleth* could do, rehash what God's prophets had said time and time again? Couldn't he come up with something new?

Don't be silly. After all, he told us way back in the first chapter, "there is nothing new under the sun."[310] The source of fulfillment for you and me is no different than it was for Samuel, or Joshua, or Moses. No different than it was for Adam and Eve. Meaning and satisfaction are found only in remembering the One who rewards you: "For God will bring every deed into judgment, including every hidden thing, whether it is good or evil."[311]

Ecclesiastes ends in language strikingly similar to the following words of Jesus, found in the last chapter of the last book of the Bible:

> Behold, I am coming soon! My reward is with me, and I
> will give to everyone according to what he has done.[312]

Whatever your life is like now, it will not always be that way. If you are living a daily struggle, if you are plagued by illness of the body or mind, it will not always be that way. If you feel crushed under a load of debt, it will not always be that way. If you feel like you've borne more than your share of disappointments and grief, it will not always be that way. No matter what hurts or hardship you are enduring now, it will not always be that way. God will bring every deed into judgment, good or evil, seen and unseen.

There will come a day—possibly soon—when your earthly journey ends, and all the things you pursued with your time, attention, life, and effort will be gone. No more money, or need for money. No more job, no more career. No more homework, no more school. No boats, TVs, concerts, restaurants, or sporting events. No status or position to think about. None of that will matter then . . . just as none of it matters now.

What matters, both then and now, is your posture toward the One who rewards you.

One Necessary Thing

I keep coming back to an incident recorded in Luke's Gospel. It may be familiar to you. If it is, I hope you won't skip over any of it, because it is the perfect scene to ponder after reading and studying *Qoheleth*'s treatise on life and meaning:

> As they went on their way, Jesus entered a village. And a woman named Martha welcomed him into her house. And she had a sister called Mary, who sat at the Lord's feet and listened to his teaching. But Martha was distracted with much serving. And she went up to him and said, "Lord, do you not care that my sister has left me to serve alone? Tell her then to help me." But the Lord answered her, "Martha, Martha, you are anxious and troubled about many things, but one thing is necessary. Mary has chosen the good portion, which will not be taken away from her."[313]

Luke tells us in verse 38 that it was Martha who welcomed Jesus into her house. This gathering was apparently her idea from the start. We don't know if Martha was married. We don't know if her sister Mary was a younger sister. We don't know if Mary's role in the household was a subordinate one to Martha. We just know that Martha invited

Jesus in, and then Mary "sat at the Lord's feet and listened to his teaching," while Martha "was distracted with much serving."   •

Notice that. Luke says Martha "was distracted with much serving." How can he say that? Martha was in charge. She extended the invitation. She apparently set the agenda. And she had clearly decided that water had to be pumped, bread had to be baked, wine had to be poured, and maybe even some meat and vegetables had to be roasted. But Luke says she "was distracted."

From what? Not from *her* agenda. And probably not from what the neighbors—maybe even social convention—would have dictated. But she was distracted . . . from what really mattered.

When Martha complained to Jesus that Mary wasn't playing by her rules, he said, "Martha, Martha, you are anxious and troubled about many things, but one thing is necessary. Mary has chosen the good portion, which will not be taken away from her."[314]

One thing is necessary, he said.

One thing.

One thing really matters.

Martha was missing it.

We know nothing about her motivation. Maybe she was putting on a show. Maybe it was about status for her. Maybe she was a bit of a workaholic. Maybe she was motivated by success; maybe she had a catering business and figured this would be great advertising. Maybe working in the kitchen was her "love language." Or maybe something else entirely was going on.

In any case, Martha missed what Mary got. Mary found her fulfillment in Jesus. She was happy to sit at his feet and absorb his teaching. She was focused on being in his presence and soaking up his words. That's what mattered to her.

Mary embodied *Qoheleth*'s wisdom:

Honor God and obey his commands,

because this is all people must do.[315]

Respect and obey God!
This is what life
      is all about.[316]

Worship God and keep God's commandments because
this is what everyone must do.[317]

And Jesus said that Mary had chosen wisely and promised that "it
will not be taken away from her."[318]

Nor will it ever be taken from you. Honor God. Live to love and
please the One who rewards you. That is what matters. Everything
else is a meaningless distraction.

God alone suffices.

———— ⌇ ————

"*O Sovereign Lord! You made the heavens and earth by your strong hand and powerful arm. Nothing is too hard for you! You show unfailing love to thousands, but you also bring the consequences of one generation's sin upon the next. You are the great and powerful God, the LORD of Heaven's Armies. You have all wisdom and do great and mighty miracles. You see the conduct of all people, and you give them what they deserve.*"[319]

Lord, you are the one who made me. I have no right to myself. You are my Creator, and you created me to be happy only in you. I acknowledge you as the one essential ingredient for a truly satisfying life. I will listen to you. I will respond to you. I will submit to you and follow you, giving you my energy and vitality while I still have those things to give.

You hold my life. I am in your hands. You alone determined when my life would begin, and you alone determine when it will end. And you alone will impart whatever reward awaits me. But I pray, when that day comes, that I will be able, like Qoheleth, *to say "I did my best, I pursued a godly purpose, and I gave it all I had." Until then, help me to focus my best efforts, energies, and attentions on one necessary thing, the only essential: you.*

In Jesus' name, amen.

Group
Study Guide

Introduction to Group Studies

The outlines on the following pages are provided for those who choose to read this book and share it with others as part of a small group study. They are intended for easy facilitation, even for those who have never led a group study before. They also require minimal preparation ahead of time—other than that particular week's reading in *Life Stinks . . . and Then You Die*, there is nothing to obtain or prepare before each session.

These outlines are intended for roughly sixty-minute sessions (the actual length will, of course, depend on the number of people and the amount of discussion and participation in a group). The outline is a suggestion; each group's facilitator should feel free to adapt the questions as desired. The following are offered as general guidelines.

Encourage everyone to follow along. Some people find it easier to participate if they know where the discussion is going. So encourage all the group members to bring their own copies of *Life Stinks . . . and Then You Die (Living Well in a Sick World)* and a Bible to the study sessions and even follow along in the study notes at the back of the book. If your group members feel comfortable doing so, you may even wish to rotate facilitators from week to week or take turns asking the questions in each session.

Don't be afraid of silence. When a question is asked, give participants time to think; silence can encourage a more thoughtful response. After ample time for thought has been allowed, signal for someone to speak up by saying, "Anybody?" or "Go ahead and express what you're thinking."

Let discussion follow its own path (without letting the group stray too far). You don't need to be in a hurry to move to the next question in the study notes, but be careful not to let the group stray into areas not related to the topic of discussion.

Feel free to follow a comment with another question. After someone has made an observation, ask such things as, "Can you think of an example?" "Anyone react to that?" or "Anyone have a different perspective?"

Don't feel obligated to ask all (or exclusively) the questions in the study notes. If your group's time is limited, highlight the questions you wish to ask. Add questions that occur to you. Encourage others to ask their own questions or add their own observations.

Group Study 1 Chapter One

Life's Just a Bowl of Cherries. Rotten Cherries.

1. Open in prayer.
2. Who is the wisest person you've ever met? (Go around the room, letting everyone answer briefly.)
3. Have someone read aloud: We are going to study together the book of Ecclesiastes, which is attributed to King Solomon. Here is what the book *Life Stinks . . . and Then You Die* says about him:

   He lived roughly one thousand years before the birth of Jesus Christ. His father was a king. And not just any king, but a man who molded a kingdom out of a bunch of fractious tribes and warring factions. The father's name was David; the son was given the name Solomon. The father was a shepherd, a poet, and a warrior; the son's very name was "peace," a form of the word *shalom*.

   Upon the death of King David, Solomon became the king in Jerusalem, sometime around 967 BC. He reigned for forty years, presiding over a period in Israel's history that is routinely called the "Golden Age." His kingdom extended from the Euphrates River in present-day Syria to the Arabian Desert and the Gulf of Aqaba in the south. His crowning achievement was the construction of the Temple in Jerusalem. He was renowned for his wisdom, wealth, and accomplishment, some of which is described in 1 Kings 4:25–34.

4. Read 1 Kings 4:25–34 together.

5. Which part of Solomon's "résumé" is most impressive to you? Which is least impressive?

6. What parts of Solomon's "résumé" do you think most qualify him to write a Bible book about life and the pursuit of happiness?

7. From what you know of the book of Ecclesiastes already (if anything), which of the following descriptions do you think is appropriate or accurate?

    *   "Disjointed in construction, obscure in vocabulary, and often cryptic in style." (George S. Hendry)
    *   "'An enigma' and an 'arsenal' for attacks against the Bible as God's Word." (F. C. Jennings)
    *   "The truest of all books . . . the fine-hammered steel of woe." (Herman Melville)
    *   "The greatest single piece of writing I have ever known." (Thomas Wolfe)

8. If there were a book in the Bible about your life—and your pursuit of happiness—what would it be called? How would it be described?

9. How has God used your life (to date) to teach something to the people around you?

10. How do you want God to use your life to help others in the future?

11. Any other questions or comments?

12. Close in prayer.

Group Study 2 Chapter 2

What Goes Around, Goes Around

1. Open in prayer.
2. What's (a) your favorite song, and (b) the saddest song you can think of? (Go around the room, letting everyone answer briefly.)
3. Read Ecclesiastes 1:1–11 together.
4. The Hebrew word for "meaningless" (v. 2) can also mean "breath" or "vapor." How does that help your understanding of what the author means?
5. What do you think the phrase "under the sun" (vv. 3, 9) means? What do you think it tells you about the author's perspective?
6. How does your labor compare to the earth's cycles (vv. 3–7)?
7. What is the theme of verses 9–11? Do you agree or disagree with the author's observation?
8. Read Ecclesiastes 1:12–18 together.
9. This book's author summarizes the message of Ecclesiastes 1 as "nothing changes," "nothing satisfies," "nothing is new," and "nothing lasts." Do you agree? Why or why not?
10. Can you think of any instances where more knowledge has caused you more sorrow, as the author of Ecclesiastes says in verse 18?
11. Does it surprise you that God (working through Jewish scholars and the Christian church) would have allowed the words of Ecclesiastes 1 into the Bible, his Word? Why or why not?
12. How do you think God wants us to view Ecclesiastes 1?
13. How do you think God wants us to respond after we read Ecclesiastes 1?

14. If Ecclesiastes 1, like all of God's Word, is supposed to help you draw closer to God, how might it do that?
15. Any other questions or comments?
16. Close in prayer.

Group Study 3 Chapter 3

The Faster I Go, the Behinder I Get

1. Open in prayer.
2. What's the fastest speed (or most pronounced sensation of going fast) you've ever experienced? (Go around the room, letting everyone answer briefly.)
3. Do you identify with the title of this week's chapter ("The Faster I Go, the Behinder I Get")? Why or why not?
4. Read Ecclesiastes 2:1–26 together.
5. In those verses, the author of Ecclesiastes says he found the pursuit of pleasure, prosperity, education, and work to be meaningless and empty. Do you agree? Why or why not?
6. Ecclesiastes 2 ends with the first of six "conclusions" the author offers throughout his book, saying:

   A person can do nothing better than to eat and drink and find satisfaction in their own toil. This too, I see, is from the hand of God, for without him, who can eat or find enjoyment? To the person who pleases him, God gives wisdom, knowledge and happiness, but to the sinner he gives the task of gathering and storing up wealth to hand it over to the one who pleases God. This too is meaningless, a chasing after the wind. (Eccl. 2:24–26)

   Do you agree or disagree with his conclusion—and why?

7. The author of *Life Stinks . . . and Then You Die* suggests that the following Bible verses relate to each other:

   Ask God, who gives generously to all without finding fault, and it will be given to you. (James 1:5b)

> Go after God, who piles on all the riches we could ever manage. (1 Tim. 6:18, *The Message*)

> To the person who pleases him, God gives wisdom, knowledge and happiness. (Eccl. 2:26a)

> Do you agree that they are related? If so, in what ways?

8. Which of the author's "meaningless" pursuits most easily distracts you from the pursuit of God: Pleasure? Prosperity/wealth? Education? Work? Something else?

9. Does Ecclesiastes 2 suggest any changes you'd like to see in your life? If so, what?

10. How can this group support or encourage you in pursuing those changes?

11. Any other questions or comments?

12. Close in prayer.

Group Study 4 Chapter 4

Getting Dizzy in the "Circle of Life"

1. Open in prayer.
2. What kind of partygoer are you? (Go around the room, letting everyone answer briefly.)

   (a) party thrower?   (b) party animal?   (c) party pooper?
   (d) wallflower?   (e) hostess helper?   (f) other _____

3. Read Ecclesiastes 3:1–8 together.
4. In this poetic depiction of life's cycles, do you think the writer is prescribing what to do or describing what is? Why do you think so?
5. Do you think verses 1–8 are "important information"? Why or why not?
6. How does your life compare to this list?
7. What "times" are you in right now?
8. Read Ecclesiastes 3:9–15 together.
9. What do you think is the "burden" God has laid on humans (v. 10)?
10. What do you think it means that God has "made everything beautiful in its time" (v. 11)?
11. What do you think it means that God has set eternity in the human heart (v. 11)?
12. Read Ecclesiastes 3:16–22 together.
13. Do you think we're intended to agree with everything in this passage? Why or why not?
14. The author of this book suggests four ways to apply this chapter to our lives:
    Cultivate the faith to accept God's timing (vv. 1–8)

Cultivate the wisdom to accomplish God's priorities (vv. 9–15)
Cultivate the patience to await God's judgment (vv. 16–17)
Cultivate the hope to anticipate God's reward (vv. 18–22)

Which of those do you think you can best apply to your life today? This week? How will you do that?

15. Any other questions or comments?
16. Close in prayer.

Group Study 5 Chapter 5

The Smarter I Get, the Less I Know

1. Open in prayer.
2. Describe the most memorable worship experience you've ever had. It can be memorable for being powerful, funny, strange, life-changing, etc. (Go around the room, letting everyone answer briefly.)
3. This week's chapter in *Life Stinks . . . and Then You Die* covered the content of Ecclesiastes 4:1–5:20. We're going to focus in on just seven verses of that passage, from Chapter Five.
4. Read Ecclesiastes 5:1–7 together.
5. What do you think it means in verse 1 when it says, "Guard your steps when you go to the house of God?" What does it mean to "guard your steps?" Do you think we do this today in our places of worship?
6. What do you think is meant by "the sacrifice of fools" (v. 1)?
7. What do you think is the point of verses 2–3? Do you think being "quick with your mouth" and "hasty in your heart" mean we shouldn't tell God what's really on our minds? Why or why not?
8. Do you think people still make vows to God, or are verses 4–7 outdated? Why or why not?
9. What do you think is the point of the statement, "Much dreaming and many words are meaningless" (v. 7)?
10. What do you think it means to "stand in awe of God" (v. 7 NIV 1984)?
11. Do you think these verses (Eccl. 5:1–7) are less applicable, more applicable, or about the same as when they were written? Why or why not?

12. How do you think these verses (Eccl. 5:1–7) apply to your life, your week, your worship?
13. Any other questions or comments?
14. Close in prayer.

Group Study 6 Chapter 6

Money Can't Buy Happiness, but Neither Can Poverty

1. Open in prayer.
2. If you compared your life to an item for sale at Walmart, which would it be most like and why? (Go around the room, letting everyone answer briefly.)

power tool	sofa	DVD
gray flannel pajamas	potted plant	HDTV
bottle of perfume	tennis shoes	4WD ATV
lawn ornament	jar of salsa	RV

3. The reading in *Life Stinks . . . and Then You Die* for this past week was the chapter "Money Can't Buy Happiness, but Neither Can Poverty." Can anyone summarize what you remember of the chapter?
4. Read Ecclesiastes 6:1–12 together.
5. Many people get uncomfortable when a discussion turns to the topic of money and wealth. Did you get uncomfortable as you read those verses in Ecclesiastes (or Chapter Six in *Life Stinks . . . and Then You Die*)? Why or why not?
6. Ecclesiastes 6 asks a number of questions. How many can you locate?
7. Do you think the questions are rhetorical or are they meant to suggest an answer?
8. If you think those questions are meant to be answered, how would you answer each of them?
9. Do you agree with the author of this book that we don't have to "follow" our hearts but can instead steer our hearts' desires

into improved ends and worthy pursuits, such as God and his will? Why do you agree or disagree?

10. This week's chapter in *Life Stinks . . . and Then You Die* quoted Warren W. Wiersbe: "To enjoy the gifts without the giver is idolatry, and this can never satisfy the human heart." How do you react to that statement?

11. How can you focus this week on enjoying both the giver (God) AND his gifts?

12. Any other questions or comments?

13. Close in prayer.

Group Study 7 Chapter 7

Too Soon Old, Too Late Smart

1. Open in prayer.
2. What was the most common saying or proverb in your home as you were growing up, such as "Don't cry over spilled milk" or "Cheaters never prosper"? (Go around the room, letting everyone answer briefly.)
3. The reading in *Life Stinks . . . and Then You Die* for this past week was the chapter "Too Soon Old, Too Late Smart." Can anyone summarize what you remember of the chapter?
4. While this week's reading material covered Ecclesiastes 7 and 8, we're going to focus on just a portion of those chapters.
5. Read Ecclesiastes 7:1–13.
6. In Ecclesiastes 7:1–12, the author strings together a series of proverbs. Proverbs, a literary form that's been around for thousands of years, are broad statements of things that are generally true (for example, "A stitch in time saves nine," or "Better safe than sorry"). How do you respond to the first four proverbs, in verses 1–4?
7. What do you think is the reason behind the advice given in verses 5–7?
8. Do you agree that the question posed in verse 10 is unwise? Why or why not?
9. In verses 11–12, what do you think is meant by comparing wisdom to "an inheritance"? To a "shelter"? Do you think wisdom really does preserve life and, if so, how? If not, why not?

10. Can you think of a time in your life when wisdom has been an inheritance, a shelter, or a life preserver for you? If so, describe it.

11. Ecclesiastes 7:13 is one of the three questions Chapter Seven of *Life Stinks . . . and Then You Die* emphasized. Why do you think it is important to "consider what God has done" and ponder "who can straighten what he has made crooked"?

12. Is there any area of your life right now where you feel the need for wisdom? If so, can you share it with the group? If someone has shared, does anyone in the group have any nugget of wisdom to share?

13. Any other questions or comments?

14. Close in prayer.

Group Study 8 Chapter 8

Live Every Day as if It's Your Last;
Someday You'll Be Right

1. Open in prayer.
2. What is the closest you've ever come to dying? (Go around the room, letting everyone answer briefly.)
3. Read Ecclesiastes 9:1–10.
4. In verses 1–6, the writer talks a lot about dying. Do you think he's trying to be depressing? If not, why is he saying such depressing things?
5. Would your life change for the better—or worse—if you heard or read Ecclesiastes 9:1–6 every morning before you started your day?
6. This past week's reading in *Life Stinks . . . and Then You Die* summarized the message of Ecclesiastes 9:1–6 as, "Live with the end in mind." Do you think that's a positive or negative way to live?
7. This past week's reading also summarized the message of Ecclesiastes 9:7–8 as, "Live—now!—with relish." Is that a message you need to hear? Why or why not?
8. This week's chapter summarized the message of Ecclesiastes 9:9 as, "Prioritize the people in your life." Do you think that's a fair way to interpret verse 9? Why or why not?
9. This week's reading in *Life Stinks . . . and Then You Die* summarized the message of Ecclesiastes 9:10 as, "Make the most of every moment, every breath." Do you know anyone who lives that way? If so, describe them.
10. On a scale of 1–10 (10 being highest), how would you rate yourself in the following areas?

- Living with the end in mind
- Living—now!—with relish
- Prioritizing the people in your life
- Making the most of every moment, every breath God gives you

11. Do these verses (Eccl. 9:1–10) suggest any changes you'd like to see in your life? If so, what?
12. How can this group support or encourage you in pursuing those changes?
13. Any other questions or comments?
14. Close in prayer.

Group Study 9

Life Is Like a Box of Chocolates; It Can Be Sweet, but It Can Make You Sick, Too

1. Open in prayer.
2. If you could choose between receiving a box of chocolates, a flower bouquet, a puppy, or theater tickets as a gift, which would you choose? (Go around the room, letting everyone answer briefly.)
3. Read Ecclesiastes 9:11.
4. The author of *Life Stinks . . . and Then You Die* suggests that one lesson to take from this verse is to "learn to expect the unexpected." Are there other ways you could apply this verse?
5. Read Ecclesiastes 9:13–17.
6. One way to apply these verses is to "learn to be content in obscurity and adversity." How much of a challenge is that for you?
7. Read Ecclesiastes 10:1–4.
8. The author of *Life Stinks . . . and Then You Die* suggests that one way to apply these verses is to "learn to be faithful in all things," and he lists four specific kinds of faithfulness:

   - be faithful in the little things of life
   - be faithful in your thought life
   - be faithful one step at a time
   - be faithful under fire

   Which of these do you find to be easiest? Hardest? Which is the most urgent need of your life right now?

9. Read Ecclesiastes 10:8–12.

10. One way to apply this series of proverbs is to "learn from the example of others." Do you tend to more easily learn from people's positive examples, or do you more readily learn what not to do from the example of others?

11. If these verses (Eccl. 9:11–10:15), like all of God's Word, are supposed to help you draw closer to God, how might they do that? How can they affect your life this week?

12. Any other questions or comments?

13. Close in prayer.

Group Study 10

Chapter 10

Living Well Is the Best Revenge

1. Open in prayer.
2. Choose one of the following questions to answer. (Go around the room, letting everyone answer briefly.)

   - Have you ever quit a job because of a boss? What made the boss hard to work for?
   - What is the worst investment (time, money, effort, etc.) you ever made? Why?
   - Describe the oldest person you've ever known personally.

3. This past week's reading in *Life Stinks . . . and Then You Die* focused on Ecclesiastes 10:16–11:10. Can anyone summarize what you remember of the chapter or what affected you the most?
4. Read Ecclesiastes 10:16–20.
5. According to *Life Stinks . . . and Then You Die*, these verses describe the wisdom of "living responsibly." What do you see them saying about living responsibly?
6. Read Ecclesiastes 11:1–6.
7. These verses describe the wisdom of "living generously." What do you think they say about living generously?
8. Read Ecclesiastes 11:7–10.
9. Those verses describe the wisdom of "living thoughtfully" (that is, living with thoughtful awareness). What do those verses say about living thoughtfully?
10. Of those three ways of life—living responsibly, generously, and thoughtfully—in which area would you say your life is strongest? Weakest? Why?

11. Speaking of living with thoughtful awareness, are you pretty much the person you were five or ten years ago? If not, describe (briefly) how you're different.

12. Again, speaking of living with thoughtful awareness, are you the person you hope to be by the time you die? If not, how do you hope to change by that time?

13. Any other questions or comments?

14. Close in prayer.

Group Study 11 Chapter 11

Growing Old Is Mandatory;
Growing Up Is Optional

1. Open in prayer.
2. What would you like your last words to be? (Go around the room, letting everyone answer briefly.)
3. The verses in Ecclesiastes 12 are the last words of *Qoheleth*, or King Solomon, on the subject of life, meaning, and happiness. Let's read the whole chapter together in this, our final study.
4. Read Ecclesiastes 12:1–14.
5. What are your thoughts after reading and/or hearing those words?
6. In Ecclesiastes 12:1–5, the author portrays old age symbolically and creatively. Why do you think he did it that way?
7. Which of those word pictures of old age hits home most for you? Why?
8. Ecclesiastes 12:6–8 depicts the end of life with four striking images. What are they?
9. Which of the following do you think those four images portray most vividly?

> life is priceless   life is fragile   life can end suddenly
> life is meaningless   death is sad   death is irreversible

10. The author of *Life Stinks . . . and Then You Die* summarizes this chapter's message in three phrases: remember who made you, remember who holds you, and remember who rewards you. Which of those phrases means the most to you, and why?
11. The author of *Life Stinks . . . and Then You Die* also compares the final words of Ecclesiastes to a passage in Luke's Gospel,

which parallels somewhat the single focus of *Qoheleth*'s conclusion. So we are going to conclude our study by reading that passage.

12. Read Luke 10:38–42.

13. Before we close in prayer, let's take a few moments to bow in silence and meditate on Jesus' words. Hear them as Jesus' words to you, and in the silence respond to them: "You are anxious and troubled about many things, but one thing is necessary" (Luke 10:41b–42a ESV).

14. Close in prayer.

Notes

Chapter 1: Life Is Just a Bowl of Cherries. Rotten Cherries.

1   Bob Thiele and George David Weiss, "What a Wonderful World," 1967, Memory Lane Music Group, Carlin Music Corp., and Bug Music, Inc.

2   1 Kings 4:25–34 NLT.

3   George S. Hendry, "Ecclesiastes," *The New Bible Commentary: Revised* (London: Inter–Varsity Press, 1970), 570.

4   F. C. Jennings, *Old Groans and New Songs: Being Meditations on the Book of Ecclesiastes* (London: S. Bagster and Sons, Ltd., 1920), 1.

5   Herman Melville, *Moby Dick* (New York: Pocket Books, 1999), 424–425.

6   Thomas Wolfe, *You Can't Go Home Again* (New York: Scribner, 2011), 628.

7   A. F. Harper, "Ecclesiastes," *Beacon Bible Commentary* (Kansas City: Beacon Hill Press, 1967), 549.

8   Charles R. Swindoll, *Living on the Ragged Edge* (Waco: Word Books, 1985), 17.

9   Ecclesiastes 1:1.

10   Hendry, 570.

11   Ronald B. Allen, "Ecclesiastes," *Nelson's New Illustrated Bible Commentary* (Nashville: Thomas Nelson, 1999), 779.

12   John Paterson, *The Book That Is Alive* (New York: Charles Scribner and Sons, 1954), 120.

13   Swindoll, 16.

Chapter 2: What Goes Around, Goes Around

14   Ecclesiastes 1:1.

15   Ecclesiastes 1:1 GW.

16   Ecclesiastes 1:1, *The Message*.

17   Ecclesiastes 1:1 GNT.

18   Ecclesiastes 1:2.

19   Norman Vincent Peale, *The Power of Positive Thinking* (Norwalk, CT: The C. R. Gibson Company, 1956), 1.

20   Napoleon Hill, *Think and Grow Rich* (New York: Tribeca Books, 2012), 9.

21   Dr. Wayne D. Dyer, *Pulling Your Own Strings* (New York: Thomas Y. Crowell Company, 1978), 3.

22   Ecclesiastes 1:2 CEB.

23   Ecclesiastes 1:2 CEV.

24   Ecclesiastes 1:2 GNT, NCV.

25   Ecclesiastes 1:2 HCSB.

26   Ecclesiastes 1:2 *The Message.*

27   Genesis 4.

28   Genesis 4:3 (italics added).

29   Ecclesiastes 1:3–7.

30   Tom Brokaw, *The Greatest Generation* (New York: Random House, 1998), xxxviii.

31   Joni Mitchell, "Woodstock" ©1969 Siquomb Publishing Corp. (BMI). From the album *Ladies of The Canyon.*

32   Joni Mitchell, "The Circle Game" ©1966, Copyright Renewed, Crazy Crow Music (BMI).
From the album *Ladies of The Canyon.*

33   Ecclesiastes 1:8.

34   Ecclesiastes 1:9–10.

35   Rudyard Kipling, "The Holy War," *Kipling: Poems* (New York: Everyman's Library, 2007), 187.

36   Ecclesiastes 1:11.

37   Ecclesiastes 1:12–18.

38   James 3:10.

39   Philip Yancey, *Prayer* (Grand Rapids: Zondervan Publishing House, 2006), 42.

40   Ecclesiastes 1:14.

41   Swindoll, 16.

42   "This World," words and music by Aaron Tate, © 1994 Cumbee Road Music.

Chapter 3: The Faster I Go, the Behinder I Get

43   Genesis 8:22.

44   Anastasia Toufexis, in "Drowsy America," *Time Magazine*, December 17, 1990, v136 n26, 78.

45   William Shakespeare, *Hamlet* (Act IV, Scene V, Line 78).

46   "Pace of life speeds up as study reveals we're walking faster than ever," by Fiona MacRae, *Mail Online* (http://www.dailymail.co.uk/sciencetech/article–452046/Pace–life–speeds–study–reveals–walking–faster–ever.html).

47   Ecclesiastes 2:1–11.

48   Andrea Canning and Jennifer Pereira, "Parents Drop Lavish Amounts on Over-the-Top Kids' Birthday Bashes," Feb. 21, 2011, http://abcnews.go.com/GMA/parents-spend-big-bucks-outrageous-kids-birthday-parties/storynew?id=12961352#.UdLyN9jhdaM.

49   "Spending on Children's Parties Holds Strong Despite Weak Economy," South Norwalk, CT (PRWEB), March 6, 2012, http://www.prweb.com/releases/GigMasters/KidsPartyTrends/prweb9253428.htm.

50   Proverbs 17:22.

51   Ecclesiastes 2:2 *The Message.*

52   "The Swelling McMansion Backlash," by Christopher Solomon, MSN Real Estate, http://realestate.msn.com/article.aspx?cp–documentid=13107733.

53   U.S. Census Bureau report, http://www.census.gov/construction/chars/highlights.html.

54   Tim Kasser, quoted in "The American Nightmare," by Lauren Sandler, *Psychology Today,* April 2011, 77.

55   Frederick Charles Jennings, *Old Groans and New Songs* (New York: Loizeaux Brothers, 1946), 29.

56   Ecclesiastes 2:12–16.

57   Ecclesiastes 2:12b.

58   Ecclesiastes 2:14.

59   Malcolm Muggeridge, *Jesus Rediscovered* (New York: Doubleday & Co., 1969), 101.

60   Ecclesiastes 2:17–23.

61   Ecclesiastes 2:17.

62   1 Peter 2:9.

63   Ecclesiastes 2:19b.

64   Quoted in Warren W. Wiersbe, *Be Satisfied* (Wheaton, IL: Victor Books, 1990), 42.

65   Ecclesiastes 2:18–19, 21.

66   2:24–26; 3:12–15, 22; 5:18–20; 8:15; 9:7–10; and 11:9–10.

67   Ecclesiastes 2:24–26.

68   Ecclesiastes 2:24a.

69   James 1:5.

70   1 Timothy 6:18 *The Message.*

71   Ecclesiastes 2:26a.

72   Leonard Sweet, *Soul Salsa* (Grand Rapids: Zondervan Publishers, 2000), 100.

73   Sweet, 101.

Chapter 4: Getting Dizzy in the "Circle of Life"

74   The *Megilloth* are Ruth, Lamentations, Ecclesiastes, Esther, and Song of Solomon, read on (respectively) Shavuot (Feast of Weeks), Ninth of Ab (commemorating the fall of Jerusalem), Sukkot (Feast of Tabernacles), Purim, and Passover.

75   Wayne H. Peterson, "Ecclesiastes," *The Broadman Bible Commentary* (Nashville: The Baptist Sunday School Board, 1973), 103.

76   Ecclesiastes 1:14.

77   Ecclesiastes 3:1–8.

78   Sheldon Kopp, *An End to Innocence* (New York: Bantam Books, 1978), 3.

79   Psalm 31:15.

80   Job 2:10.

81   Norman Gimbel and Charles Fox, "Happy Days." Copyright 1974, Bruin Music Company (BMI).

82   Joe South, "Rose Garden." Copyright 1967, Lowery Music Co., Inc.

83   Ecclesiastes 3:1.

84   Jacques Ellul, *The Reason for Being: A Meditation on Ecclesiastes* (Grand Rapids: Wm. B. Eerdmans Publishing Co., 1990), 225.

85   Anatole France, quoted in *You Gotta Keep Dancing* by Tim Hansel (Elgin, IL: David C. Cook, 1985), 72.

86   Ellul, 234.

87   Malcolm Muggeridge, *A Twentieth Century Testimony* (Nashville: Thomas Nelson Publishers, 1978).

88   Ecclesiastes 3:9–15.

89   Ecclesiastes 2:18–19a.

90   Ecclesiastes 3:14.

91   Ecclesiastes 3:16–17.

92   Romans 2:6–8 NIV 1984.

93   Matthew 13:24–30 NIV 1984.

94   Ecclesiastes 3:17b.

95   Ecclesiastes 3:18–22.

96   Psalm 23:6 NIV 1984.

97   Ecclesiastes 3:11b NLT.

98   Ecclesiastes 3:21.

99   1 Corinthians 13:12a KJV.

100 Hebrews 11:1 NIV 1984.

101 Thornton Wilder, *Our Town: A Play in Three Acts* (New York: Harper Perennial Modern Classics, 2003), 87–88.

102 Ecclesiastes 3:11b NLT.

103 Ecclesiastes 3:22.

104 Psalm 23:6.

105 Luke 22:42.

106 Ecclesiastes 3:14.

107 Romans 2:7.

108 Romans 2:8.

109 Ecclesiastes 3:17.

110 Psalm 23:6.

Chapter 5: The Smarter I Get, the Less I Know

111 Ecclesiastes 4:1–8.

112 Bob Dylan, "My Back Pages" © 1964 by Warner Bros. Music. Copyright renewed 1992 by Special Rider Music. Used by permission.

113 Ecclesiastes 4:9–12.

114 Ecclesiastes 4:12.

115 Bill Hybels, *Courageous Leadership* (Grand Rapids: Zondervan Publishers, 2002), 22–23.

116 Ecclesiastes 4:13–16.

117 Ecclesiastes 5:1–7.

118 Ecclesiastes 5:8–17.

119 Ecclesiastes 5:9.

120 Bob Lind, "Elusive Butterfly," © 1965 and 1966 by Metric Music Co.

121 Ecclesiastes 5:11a.

122 Ecclesiastes 5:15.

123 Ecclesiastes 5:18–20.

124 1 Timothy 6:6.

125 Luke 16:13.

126 1 Thessalonians 5:18 KJV.

127 Luke 12:33 NIRV.

Chapter 6: Money Can't Buy Happiness, but Neither Can Poverty

128 1 Chronicles 22:14.

129 1 Kings 10:14.

130 Ecclesiastes 6:1–2.

131 Ecclesiastes 6:2b.

132 Ecclesiastes 6:2a.

133 Henry David Thoreau, *Walden* (Oxford: Oxford University Press, 2008), 48.

134 George Herbert, Charles Cowden Clark (editor), *The Poetical Works of George Herbert and The Synagogue by C. Harvey* (Whitefish, MT: Kessenger Publishing, 2007), 68.

135 Jeremiah 17:9.

136 1 Corinthians 2:16.

137 Ecclesiastes 6:2a.

138 Ecclesiastes 5:19.

139 A. W. Tozer (compiled by Gerald B. Smith), *The Tozer Pulpit, Vol. 1* (Camp Hill, PA: Christian Publications, 1994), Book IV, 115–17.

140 Warren W. Wiersbe, *Be Satisfied* (Colorado Springs: David C. Cook, 1990), 88.

141 "Saint Vincent Pallotti," *Saints.SQPN.com*. 21 April 2012. Web. 26 January 2013. <http://saints.sqpn.com/saint–vincent–pallotti/>

142 Psalm 37:4 ESV.

143 Philippians 4:10–12.

144 Ecclesiastes 6:3–9.

145 Philippians 3:18–19 *The Message*.

146 Matthew 16:24.

147 Samuel Logan Brengle, *Helps to Holiness* (London: Salvationist Publishing and Supplies, 1955), 51, 53.

148 Luke 12:15.

149 "A man is rich in proportion to the number of things he can afford to let alone" (Henry David Thoreau, *Walden* (Oxford: Oxford University Press, 2008), 59.

150 Ecclesiastes 6:10–12.

151 Matthew 10:38–39.

152 Matthew 10:38–39 *The Message*.

153 Genesis 32:9–11.

154 Genesis 32:24–31.

155 E. Stanley Jones, *Abundant Living* (New York: Abingdon–Cokesbury Press, 1942), 31.

156 "Saint Vincent Pallotti," *Saints.SQPN.com*. 21 April 2012. Web. 26 January 2013. <http://saints.sqpn.com/saint–vincent–pallotti/>

Chapter 7: Too Soon Old, Too Late Smart

157 Jeffrey Dach, M.D., "Doctor Says Trust Me, Cigarettes Are Healthy," January 4, 2009, http://open.salon.com/blog/jeffrey_dach_md/2009/01/04/your_doctor_says_have_a_smoke_its_healthy.

158 Ibid.

159 Ecclesiastes 6:8a.

160 Ecclesiastes 6:12.

161 Ecclesiastes 7:1–10.

162 Ecclesiastes 7:11–12.

163 1 Kings 3:5b.

164 1 Kings 3:10–14

165 Ecclesiastes 7:13.

166 Isaiah 14:13b–14.

167 Ecclesiastes 7:13.

168 Ecclesiastes 7:14.

169 Ecclesiastes 7:15.

170 Ecclesiastes 7:16–18.

171 The emphasis in these verses is human effort. Self-righteousness and self-abasement are two extremes of self-centeredness. If you think you are without sin you are deceived (John 1:8) as much as if you think you are too wicked for God's grace.

172 Ecclesiastes 7:19–20.

173 Ecclesiastes 7:21–22.

174 Ecclesiastes 7:23.

175 Ecclesiastes 7:24.

176 Ecclesiastes 7:25.

177 This statement may not be as misogynistic as it sounds at first. *Qoheleth's* reference to "them all" may refer to his three hundred wives and seven hundred concubines (i.e., all "thousand" women). If that is the case, he is bemoaning his perceived lack of his ideal woman (see Proverbs 31) among "them all." Even at that, however, his statement underscores the point that however wise a man may be (or think he is), there will always be gaping holes in his "wisdom."

178 Ecclesiastes 7:26–29.

179 Ecclesiastes 7:13.

180 Ecclesiastes 7:13 NLT.

181 Proverbs 3:5–6.

182 Ecclesiastes 8:1.

183   Ecclesiastes 8:1a NLT.

184   Proverbs 1:7 TLB.

185   James 1:5a.

186   Proverbs 12:15 *The Message*.

187   Proverbs 11:14 NLT.

188   Proverbs 10:14 NIV 1984.

189   John Maxwell, *Thinking for a Change* (New York: Warner Books, 2003), 40.

190   Proverbs 28:7 *The Message*.

191   Proverbs 13:20.

192   Ecclesiastes 8:16–17.

193   Ashton Applewhite, William R. Evans III, and Andrew Frothingham, *And I Quote* (New York: St. Martin's Press, 2003), 169.

194   James 3:13.

195   Ecclesiastes 7:13 NLT.

196   James 1:5a.

197   Proverbs 13:20.

Chapter 8: Live Every Day as if It's Your Last; Someday You'll Be Right

198   Ecclesiastes 3:10–11a.

199   Ecclesiastes 3:11b.

200   Ecclesiastes 5:11a.

201   Ecclesiastes 6:7.

202   Ecclesiastes 6:11a.

203   Ecclesiastes 7:2b.

204   Ecclesiastes 12:12.

205   Ellul, 159.

206   Ecclesiastes 9:1–6.

207   Ecclesiastes 9:3b.

208   Stephen Covey, *The Seven Habits of Highly Effective People* (New York: Simon and Schuster, 1989), 96–97.

209   Frederick Buechner, *Telling Secrets* (New York: HarperCollins Publishers, 1991), 18.

210   Ecclesiastes 9:4a.

211   Ellul, 53.

212   Ecclesiastes 9:7–8.

213   Ecclesiastes 9:7a *The Message*.

214 Wiersbe, 127.

215 Ecclesiastes 9:7b.

216 Ecclesiastes 9:7b *The Message.*

217 Wilder, 108.

218 Gerhard E. Frost, *Blessed Is the Ordinary: Reflections* (Minneapolis: Winston Press, 1980).

219 Ecclesiastes 9:8.

220 Tim Hansel, quoted in Swindoll, 265.

221 Proverbs 5:18b.

222 Ecclesiastes 9:9.

223 Ecclesiastes 9:9 NLT.

224 Ecclesiastes 9:9a NLT.

225 Ecclesiastes 9:10.

226 Colossians 3:23.

227 Thoreau, 66.

228 Erma Bombeck, "If I Had My Life to Live Over," *Saturday Evening Post*, 253 Nov. 1981, 17.

229 Jerusalem Talmud, Kiddushin 4:12.

230 Charles Dickens, *Oliver Twist* (Mineola, NY: Dover Publications, 2002), 11.

231 Thoreau, 66.

Chapter 9: Life Is Like a Box of Chocolates; It Can Be Sweet, but It Can Make You Sick, Too

232 John 9:1–2.

233 Interestingly, the opening line of Groom's novel is quite different. It begins, "Let me say this: bein a idiot is no box of chocolates" (Winston Groom, *Forrest Gump* (New York: Washington Square Press, 1986), 1.

234 From a line of dialogue in a 1996 episode of *The X–Files* (http://www.quotecounterquote.com/2010/07/life–is–like–box–of–chocolates–or–maybe.html)

235 Ecclesiastes 9:11.

236 Ecclesiastes 9:12.

237 Ecclesiastes 9:13–18.

238 Ellul, 113.

239 1 Corinthians 9:1–6, 2 Corinthians 11:5.

240 2 Corinthians 4:8–9, 11:23–29.

241 Philippians 4:12–13 *The Message.*

242 Ecclesiastes 10:1–4 NIV 1984.

243 Ecclesiastes 10:1.

244 Luke 16:10 ESV.

245 Ecclesiastes 10:2 *The Message*.

246 James Allen, *As a Man Thinketh* (New York: Barnes & Noble Publishing, Inc., 1992), 11, 25.

247 Philippians 4:8b NLT.

248 Psalm 101:3, 119:37.

249 I have written in various places about my long habit of devising an annual reading plan for this very purpose. One version of it can be read on the Desperate Pastor blog (http://desperatepastor.blogspot.com); search for "annual reading plan."

250 Ecclesiastes 10:2 *The Message*.

251 Ecclesiastes 10:3.

252 Friedrich Nietzsche, *Beyond Good and Evil*, trans. Helen Zimmern (New York: Tribeca Books, 2012), 52.

253 William Shakespeare, *Hamlet, Prince of Denmark*, Act III, Scene IV, Lines 172–177.

254 Ecclesiastes 10:4.

255 Job 23:10.

256 Ecclesiastes 10:5–15.

257 Philippians 4:12–13 *The Message*.

Chapter 10: Living Well Is the Best Revenge

258 Ecclesiastes 2:10.

259 Ecclesiastes 1:14 NLT 1996.

260 Ecclesiastes 1:8a.

261 Ecclesiastes 5:15a NLT.

262 Ecclesiastes 9:12b NCV.

263 Ecclesiastes 10:16–17.

264 Ecclesiastes 10:18.

265 Ecclesiastes 10:19.

266 2 Thessalonians 3:10.

267 Ecclesiastes 10:20.

268 Ecclesiastes 11:1–2 NIV 1984.

269 Ecclesiastes 11:2a.

270 Ecclesiastes 11:3.

271   2 Corinthians 9:8, 11a NIV 1984.

272   Ecclesiastes 11:4.

273   Ecclesiastes 11:4.

274   Ecclesiastes 11:5–6.

275   Ecclesiastes 11:2b.

276   Tyler Perry, The Official Tyler Perry Fan Page, February 8, 2013 (http://www.facebook.com/thetylerperry/posts/10151549214993268).

277   Ecclesiastes 11:7–8.

278   Ecclesiastes 11:8a.

279   Ecclesiastes 11:9–10.

280   Francis Chan, *Crazy Love* (Colorado Springs: David C. Cook Publishing, 2008), 47.

281   Chan, 46.

Chapter 11: Growing Old Is Mandatory; Growing Up Is Optional

282   Abigail Brenner, M.D., "Five Ways to Find Closure from the Past: Actions That Help You Move Into Your Future," *Psychology Today*, April 6, 2011 (http://www.psychologytoday.com/blog/in–flux/201104/5–ways–find–closure–the–past).

283   Ecclesiastes 11:9–10.

284   Abigail Brenner, M.D., "Five Ways to Find Closure from the Past: Actions That Help You Move Into Your Future," *Psychology Today*, April 6, 2011 (http://www.psychologytoday.com/blog/in–flux/201104/5–ways–find–closure–the–past).

285   Ellul, 107.

286   Ecclesiastes 12:1a.

287   Swindoll, 342.

288   Adam Clarke, *Clarke's Commentary*, Vol. III (New York: Abingdon–Cokesbury Press, n.d.), 836.

289   Ecclesiastes 12:1–5.

290   Wiersbe, 153–154.

291   Ecclesiastes 12:6–7.

292   Zechariah 4:2a.

293   Ecclesiastes 12:7b.

294   Ecclesiastes 12:8.

295   Ecclesiastes 1:2.

296 *Qoheleth*'s statements, "Who knows if the spirit of man rises upward"
and "the spirit returns to God who gave it" do not necessarily indicate a wavering
belief in eternity. When he speaks of the spirit returning to God, he is picturing
a reversal of Genesis 2:7 (i.e., as God formed humans from dust and breathed life
into them, death returns humans to dust, and their spirit departs).

297 Ecclesiastes 12:9–12.

298 Ecclesiastes 12:9b.

399 Ecclesiastes 12:9b ESV.

300 Ecclesiastes 12:9c.

301 Ecclesiastes 12:11b.

302 Ecclesiastes 12:12b.

303 1 Kings 4:32 NLT.

304 2 Timothy 4:7.

305 Ecclesiastes 12:13–14.

306 Swindoll, 342.

307 Deuteronomy 10:12–13 NIV 1984.

308 Joshua 24:14.

309 1 Samuel 12:24.

310 Ecclesiastes 1:9b.

311 Ecclesiastes 12:14.

312 Revelation 22:12.

313 Luke 10:38–42 ESV.

314 Luke 10:41–42 ESV.

315 Ecclesiastes 12:13b NCV.

316 Ecclesiastes 12:13b CEV.

317 Ecclesiastes 12:13b CEB.

318 Luke 10:42b.

319 Jeremiah 32:17–19 NLT.